Salvador Dalí
A Captivating Guide to the Life of a Famous Spanish Painter Who Is Known for His Surrealist Paintings and Flamboyant Personality

© Copyright 2020

All Rights Reserved. No part of this book may be reproduced in any form without permission in writing from the author. Reviewers may quote brief passages in reviews.
    Disclaimer: No part of this publication may be reproduced or transmitted in any form or by any means, mechanical or electronic, including photocopying or recording, or by any information storage and retrieval system, or transmitted by email without permission in writing from the publisher.
    While all attempts have been made to verify the information provided in this publication, neither the author nor the publisher assumes any responsibility for errors, omissions or contrary interpretations of the subject matter herein.
    This book is for entertainment purposes only. The views expressed are those of the author alone, and should not be taken as expert instruction or commands. The reader is responsible for his or her own actions.
    Adherence to all applicable laws and regulations, including international, federal, state and local laws governing professional licensing, business practices, advertising and all other aspects of doing business in the US, Canada, UK or any other jurisdiction is the sole responsibility of the purchaser or reader.
    Neither the author nor the publisher assumes any responsibility or liability whatsoever on the behalf of the purchaser or reader of these materials. Any perceived slight of any individual or organization is purely unintentional.

Free Bonus from Captivating History (Available for a Limited time)

Hi History Lovers!

Now you have a chance to join our exclusive history list so you can get your first history ebook for free as well as discounts and a potential to get more history books for free! Simply visit the link below to join.

Captivatinghistory.com/ebook

Also, make sure to follow us on Facebook, Twitter and Youtube by searching for Captivating History.

Contents

INTRODUCTION 1
CHAPTER 1 - PREHISTORY TO PICASSO 3
CHAPTER 2 - FINDING THE MAGIC...9
CHAPTER 3 - GROWING WINGS..15
CHAPTER 4 - REBELLION 22
CHAPTER 5 - RISEN STAR 29
CHAPTER 6 - FAME AND ECCENTRICITY 37
CHAPTER 7 - THE BATHTUB AND THE WINDOW 45
CHAPTER 8 - FLIGHT..52
CHAPTER 9 - GOING HOME...62
CHAPTER 10 - FAREWELL TO THE MUSE..71
CHAPTER 11 - THE MARQUIS' LAST DRAWING..77
CHAPTER 12 - THE IMMORTAL MUSTACHE...84
CONCLUSION..88
LINKS TO MORE PICTURES OF FAMOUS SPANISH PAINTINGS (BY DALÍ AND OTHERS) 91
GLOSSARY..92
SOURCES 94

I have Dalínian thought: the one thing the world will never have enough of is the outrageous.
   - Salvador Dalí

Introduction

What do you think of when you hear the name Salvador Dalí? Is it a curly mustache or melting watches? Art that looks at first glance like it was painted by some great master of realism until you take a closer look and discover that the piercing details belong to dreams?

Salvador Dalí was a master of the surreal. His paintings are known as "dream-photographs": snapshots of nightmarish scenes brought to life in stunning detail. Dalí was a technical virtuoso, but unlike the grand masters he admired—like Johannes Vermeer and Diego Velázquez—he chose to use his skill to depict the unreal and the absurd. Anyone who has seen his famous painting of the melting watches, *The Persistence of Memory*, knows that his paintings are as confusing as they are striking.

Yet like Dalí himself, there are more to those paintings than just what's on the surface. Unlike many artists of his age, Dalí was a glamorous celebrity, and his pointy mustache has remained a symbol of art and quirkiness to this day. He was as ridiculous as his paintings, but he was also a human being.

When one begins to analyze a Dalí painting, layers upon layers of meaning manifest themselves. A soft watch becomes the human perception of time. Ants become a symbol of destruction; a burning giraffe, a premonition of war. Complicated symbolism captures profound and powerful themes upon the canvas of the strange and ridiculous. Dalí himself is much more complicated than just a funny, crazy man with wacky paintings. He lived through an era of history that was packed with challenges, and his mind was a strange place, a place filled with mystery and genius.

In this book, we take a step beyond Dalí's art and intelligence and pull back the curtain for a glimpse deep inside the psyche of the man himself. We seek out the reasons why he chose Surrealism to express himself. We probe the outward shell of his arrogant, egocentric persona and find the deepest fears and insecurities that made him human. We discover his truest love, his greatest terror, and his heartbreak over the wars that were ripping his world apart.

Salvador Dalí was a genius, an artist, a celebrity, and a pioneer. But he was also human. And this is his story.

Chapter 1 – Prehistory to Picasso

Thousands of years before history began, a barrel-chested figure stood in a cave lit by the flicker of a yellow flame. The man, if you could have called him a man, had heavy brows and sturdy legs, with a lower jaw like an anvil. There was a brutish grace in the way he moved—something heavy and muscular. He didn't move like a deer. He moved like a falling stone. Like a boulder given life.

The modern audience could be excused for thinking that the man in the cave was little more than an animal. He was heavy and hairy, with a protruding nose and a bony ridge of brow that hid deep-set brown eyes. His movement was low and loping, like something that still ran down its prey. Muscles rippled on his bare torso as he turned to face the wall, watching his shadow dance across it in the firelight. His hair and beard were wind-combed, sun-bleached, and stiff with the salt of the sea, which was so close that its roar and scent pervaded every inch of the cave.

Someday the cave where he stood would be known as the Cave of Los Aviones. The name means Aircraft Cave, and it would be discovered in southeast Spain near Cartagena. But to the man in the cave with the fire, it wasn't anywhere but home.

He felt a stirring in him. An urge that couldn't be tamed, a kind of longing to leave something behind, to express something more beautiful than his bones. He bent down and lifted a red pigment made of earth and crushed seashells. He studied the smooth cave walls and thought about everything he'd seen that day, the images chasing each other through his brain.

And then the Neanderthal began to paint.

He painted the things he knew, the shapes he loved. The hulking height of a great red bull. The tossing mane of a fleeing horse. The crouching power of a stalking predator. The more he painted, the more the Neanderthal began to paint things that he couldn't see, things he couldn't put into words, things we still can't express thousands of years later. They came out as lines and squiggles, stripes and dots, scrawled with a wild joy across the face of that cave wall. The man filled the wall with the way the smell of rain made him feel, with the keen edge of biting loss, with the sound of the sea, with the way he felt when he walked home after a successful hunt. He filled it with love and longing and fear and confusion and hope.

And when he was done, he laid his hand on the cave wall and painted pigment all around it. When he lifted his hand away, the print remained, outlined in red. It left a piece of him trapped there in the rock. It left his imprint.

* * * *

Thousands of years later, the imprints of Neanderthal hands still remain on the walls of Spanish caves, along with the rest of their haunting art. From the blindingly lifelike depictions of nature and animals to the strange shadows of their hands to the abstract marks whose meanings have long been lost, Neanderthal art is real and has been found in numerous locations in Spain. We don't know why exactly these ancient people painted on cave walls. Our imagining of the lone caveman painting his humanity on a canvas of rock may not be accurate; the Neanderthals may have had a more complicated culture than we could have ever anticipated, and art may have been an integral part of it.

The paintings of the Cave of Los Aviones and other caves like it are evidence of humanity—and not only humanity but humanity's inextricable link with art. To make art, it is implied, is to be human.

Ever since people were people, we have sought to leave an impression of ourselves upon this world, to depict something of the lives we lead. Some of us have become masters of creating art. And Spain, the birthplace and long-time home of Salvador Dalí, produced many such masters.

The Neanderthals of the Cave of Los Aviones were only the first. Spanish masters of art would only truly begin to proliferate in the 16th century when the Renaissance was at its height.

El Greco was one of the first Spanish painters to truly make his mark on the early modern world. Born Doménikos Theotokópoulos in 1541, he was originally from the Greek island of Crete. After studying in Venice, he moved to Spain, where he began to paint in earnest and became famous by his nickname, El Greco (meaning "the Greek"). The Spanish Renaissance had brought art in the country to a level hitherto undreamed of, as artists had discovered techniques that made their paintings incredibly realistic. El Greco's early works are examples of this hyper-realism. They are beautifully composed and make perfect use of techniques like proportion and light that were still comparatively new concepts when he first began to paint. Like many of his era, El Greco was deeply religious and had his earliest art education in Byzantine iconography. He would later be commissioned to paint for numerous churches.

But El Greco quickly found that his wild imagination was not content staying within the confines of tradition. A deeply devout man with a powerful personal faith, El Greco sought to express his deep feelings of devotion with more than simple realism. The more he painted, the more his art began to deviate from the real and stray into the very earliest form of abstract art, known as Mannerism. Still a far cry from the crazy colors and senseless lines of true abstract art, El Greco's paintings began to employ the use of improbable proportions, radical foreshortening, and loud, unrealistic colors. The result had a powerfully emotional effect on those who viewed it, stirring up feelings of adoration and devotion. His masterpiece, *The Burial of the Count of Orgaz*, makes use of many of these techniques. He is famously quoted as telling artists that "[you] must study the Masters but guard the original style that beats within your soul." It was this unique style that made El Greco one of Spain's most famous early painters.

Fifty years after El Greco came two more painters who would leave an indelible mark on Spanish—and global—art. These men were born just one year apart, and where El Greco deviated from tradition, these two painters were masters of classical art. The first, born in 1598, was Francisco de Zurbarán.

Zurbarán was another religious painter who produced intensely realistic works for churches and other Christian institutions. His paintings are dramatic and contemplative, with an almost melancholy quality achieved by tenebrism (the use of light in which most of the painting is wreathed in shadow, with a few parts of it being brightly lit), which show devotion to the Renaissance ideal of naturalism. King Philip IV of Spain was one of his many patrons; Zurbarán even decorated a ship for the king. Despite his early successes, though, the untimely death of Zurbarán's wife was a blow that catapulted him into depression and poverty. Zurbarán was practically destitute when he died in 1664.

One thing that Zurbarán did have to the very end was his friendship with Diego Velázquez, a contemporary artist of his who may have had even more of an effect on Spanish art. Like Zurbarán, Velázquez started out painting religious scenes, but he quickly found his niche was in portraiture. He is known for creating sympathetic, powerful portraits, bringing individuals to life with emotionally realistic images. After a six-year apprenticeship, which started when he was only eleven, Velázquez was given the opportunity to paint a portrait of Gaspar de Guzmán, the Count-Duke of Olivares; the latter recommended Velázquez to King Philip IV. He was promptly hired as a court painter, and the king decided that none other than Velázquez would ever be allowed to paint him. Intriguingly, Velázquez was not content with simply painting the members of one of the most powerful royal families in the entire world. He also painted the dwarfs who served in the king's court. To the rest of the world, these people were little more than a curiosity; to King Philip, they were simply another attraction in his sumptuous court. But Velázquez depicts them with a sympathy that reveals their humanity.

Velázquez was still working for King Philip when he died in 1660; by then, Velázquez was already almost overshadowed by the next great Spanish painter, Bartolomé Esteban Murillo. Although his name is not as well known today, in his time, Murillo was one of the most famous painters in the world. He was primarily a religious painter and did much of the work for the beautiful Seville Cathedral, attaining fame and success despite the fact that he was orphaned at the tender age of ten.

In the 18th century, a less traditional painter than Velázquez, Murillo, and Zurbarán would arise, one who would become known as the father of modern art: Francisco Goya. Starting out as another successful court painter, this time for King Charles IV, Goya was another master of realism who would later turn to a more abstract style. Unlike his predecessors, he was not working in a stable and prosperous Spanish Empire. The political climate of Goya's time was fraught with peril and oppression. The common people were being crushed beneath the unforgiving heel of the bureaucracy, and despite his position as court painter, Goya sided with them. His bitterness toward the royal family was evident in his paintings, as his portraits started to morph more and more into caricatures. Some of his later works are almost entirely abstract, with simple, grotesque shapes and dark themes such as the bloodied form of *Saturn Devouring His Son*. His dark paintings are a reflection of darker times. Goya went into exile as an old man in 1824 and continued to paint until his death four years later.

Perhaps the greatest Spanish painter of them all—arguably unrivaled both in fame and in his utterly groundbreaking work—was Pablo Picasso.

Velázquez and Goya would both serve as inspirations for the young Picasso, who was a child prodigy. His first word was "pencil," and one of his earliest paintings, *The Picador* (painted in 1890 when he was only nine years old), already shows some of the abstract elements that he would become a pioneer of. At the age of thirteen, Picasso was admitted to the Royal Academy of Fine Arts in Barcelona, where he would learn classical painting—and swiftly reject it.

Even though Picasso showed great potential as a classical artist, and admired the works of Murillo and Velázquez, he was particularly attracted to the very different style of Goya. As a young man, Picasso seemed to be on the fast track to becoming another great Spanish realism artist. Everything changed in 1898, though. Illness forced Picasso to spend a long convalescence in Catalonia, far from his family and other influences. His body recovered, and his artistic spirit was set free. Picasso was done painting what other people liked. He wanted to paint what *he* liked—and that proved to be a style that would revolutionize the world of art forever.

Picasso became the pioneer of Cubism, an abstract art technique that involves the use of geometric shapes and scrambled planes that interlock to form a strangely simple, yet poignant, image. He was also one of the first artists to use a collage as we know it today. While he was also a poet and costume designer (among other things), Picasso became famous for his gloriously unique paintings.

In fact, Picasso's paintings—and there are thousands of them—started a new era in Spanish art. It was an era of free expression, of experimenting with different techniques, of mastering more than the art of the real. Of painting not only what is seen but also what is felt. And it was into this era that another master was born: Salvador Dalí.

Chapter 2 – Finding the Magic

Illustration I: A young Salvador Dalí before growing his iconic mustache

When Salvador Dalí was born, Picasso was painting everything in blue.

The young Picasso had just experienced a great and personal loss: the death of his friend, Carles Casagemas. A fellow artist and rebel, Casagemas had shot himself over his rejection by a woman shortly after Picasso had left him in Paris and journeyed back to Barcelona. Picasso was only nineteen years old at the time. He felt somehow responsible for Casagemas' death and slipped into a turbulent depression from which some of his greatest paintings emerged, a time known as the Blue Period. Moody hues of cool colors characterized this period, and Picasso even painted Casagemas several times, often trying to depict his death scene as the young artist struggled to come to terms with what had happened.

It was 1901, and Picasso was still deep in the throes of his Blue Period when Salvador Dalí was born. Not the first Salvador Dalí, no—that was his father, a lawyer from the soles of his shoes to the top of his head. The elder Salvador was a stern, unflinching atheist, set in his ways and deeply invested in his ideas. His first son was born to Felipa Domènech Ferrés, Salvador Senior's beautiful and sweet wife. Felipa was to Salvador Senior what a flower is to a stone. She was a free-spirited, kind, and devout Catholic young woman who adored her first child.

Salvador Junior was only a baby when he was horribly gripped by a bout of gastroenteritis. In the modern day, this disease is common and often easily managed, but in 1903, this was not the case. The baby lived less than three years, dying in August 1903. His death was a crushing blow even to the impenetrable Salvador Senior, and it must have been devastating to Felipa as well.

They mourned through the winter of 1903 and into the balmy Spanish spring of 1904, and that was when Felipa's belly started to grow larger and larger. As Picasso painted blue and Spain itself grew more and more tumultuous under the pressure of a fracturing Europe, Felipa brought forth another baby boy on May 11th, 1904. Felipa and Salvador Senior were delighted with yet another boy, and what was more, the baby bore a truly uncanny resemblance to the child that they had lost. To the grieving parents, it felt like they were being given a second chance; it felt like a part of baby Salvador had returned to them. It is hardly surprising then that they elected to give the baby the same name that was borne by his stern father and his dead brother: Salvador.

Little Salvador grew up near where he was born, near the French border in Catalonia, not far from Barcelona itself—that same city where the great Picasso had first studied. Even as a small child, Salvador proved to have his eccentricities. He was temperamental, passionate, and prone to tantrums, a fact possibly exacerbated by the disunity between his parents—where Felipa was lenient, Salvador Senior was strict. The young Salvador loved his indulgent mother fiercely; however, he was not so devoted to his father.

One thing upon which Felipa and Salvador Senior agreed was evident, and it was proven to little Salvador in 1909 when he was only five years old. The two parents brought him to a very small grave. If little Salvador had been able to read, he would have seen that the headstone of the tiny grave bore the same name as he did. Facing the grave with their toddling son, Felipa and Salvador Senior solemnly told him that he was not just any child. In fact, he was the reincarnation of his deceased older brother. It's impossible to tell how much of this little Salvador understood at the time, but the moment must have stuck with him because he would cling to this memory—and believe what he'd been told—for the rest of his life.

By that time, Salvador was no longer an only child. He had a two-year-old sister, Anna Maria. And despite the disciplinarian philosophies of Salvador's father, it would appear that his childhood was not an unhappy one. He had little Anna Maria to play with, he was utterly doted on by Felipa, and when he began to show a propensity for art at an early age, his parents were both quick to encourage him. Becoming an artist, they decided, would be a suitably prosperous career for the young Salvador. In fact, he was only six years old when he created his first painting, *Landscape Near Figueras*. It's almost impossible to believe that a six-year-old child created this beautiful piece of art, a Van Gogh-esque impressionist piece featuring distant mountains that tower over trees and buildings. The colors and brushstrokes are used with a skill that one would imagine reaches far beyond the abilities of a child that age.

Three years later, when he was nine, Salvador finished his second painting, *Vilabertran*. This oil painting, like his first, is of a landscape that would have been familiar to him. It shows more advanced use of shapes and colors and depicts a peaceful scene of a home in the countryside. Although the painting has some impressionist features, it would appear that Salvador's work was becoming more and more realistic, as would be expected from a young child learning to paint. His parents may have even expected him to become a classical artist. However, a new influence would soon enter his life, one that would steer him in an entirely different direction.

In 1914, when Salvador was ten years old, his parents decided to continue encouraging his art by enrolling him in drawing school. It was around this time that Salvador met his first real-life artist: Ramon Pichot. A tall, thin, friendly Impressionist, Pichot was a friend to Picasso and quickly became a mentor to Salvador Dalí thanks to his friendship with the Dalí family, who would often go on holidays with the Pichots. Ramon mostly painted people, often in a sympathetic and sensitive style that reflected his kindly nature, and Salvador was immediately drawn to this different way of painting. Salvador had been introduced to modern art, and he loved it. His next painting, which was finished when he was only twelve years old, reflected this new influence. *Fiesta in Figueres* shows a happy, well-dressed crowd reveling under bursts of fireworks that blur in twirls of light, not unlike the stars in Van Gogh's *Starry Night*. Salvador was well on his way to becoming a modern artist.

Juan Nunez, a lecturer at the Figueres Institute and one of Salvador's very first art teachers, was another influence on Salvador, one that would pull him back toward realism. Nunez was a lover of Rembrandt and Vermeer, and he considered Velázquez to be Spain's greatest artist. Pichot had taught Salvador how to paint an impression; Nunez taught him how to paint reality. A perfectionist, Nunez insisted that Salvador learned the classical techniques, and the young artist hung on his every word. While realism was never Salvador's favorite form of art, he did learn many techniques from Nunez, techniques that would stand him in good stead as he continued on his quest to find the style that would truly inspire him. Unfortunately for Salvador, Surrealism, as we know it today, did not yet exist when he was just a boy.

The Dalís and Pichots often holidayed together at a location that would become integral to Salvador's life and his art: Cadaques. Cadaques was a small town set in a jewel-blue bay in Catalonia, complete with woods, fields, long, green hills, and a glittering expanse of sea extending into the port town itself. All of this served to inspire Dalí constantly. Cadaques' magnificent landscapes and tranquil atmosphere would serve as one of Salvador's greatest muses throughout his life, and this was already evident in his very earliest paintings.

His painting, *View of Cadaques with Shadow of Mount Pani* (1917), was inspired by one of his many trips to Cadaques with the Pichot family. This oil painting depicts a sunset in the most dazzling colors. *Port of Cadaques*, which was painted in 1919 when Salvador was fifteen years old, is similarly beautiful and deeply impressionist, showing the reflections of lights on the port at night. The year before, though, Salvador had painted a person for the first time. *Crepuscular Old Man* (1918) is an expressionist portrait of a bent, balding old man struggling along the street, and it already holds some of the dreamlike quality with which Salvador would later infuse his more advanced works.

When he was fifteen years old, Salvador's father decided that it was high time the boy's beautiful art was shared with the rest of the world. He opened the doors of their family home in Figueres to the public, holding an exhibition of Salvador's paintings and charcoal sketches, which were reported to be beautiful. It would be Salvador's first exhibition, and although it was a fairly informal family event, it was a stepping stone to greater things. Soon after, Salvador took part in his first real public exhibition in the Municipal Theater of Figueres, likely with the oil paintings mentioned above.

Like Picasso, Salvador had already proven to be a child prodigy, brilliant even in his youth. It would appear, though, that he was not an easy child to have around. Desperately indulged by his mother and constantly rebelling against his authoritarian father, Salvador had grown spoiled and difficult. His propensity for tantrums as a little boy had turned into a tendency toward violence as a teenager; he was reported to have pushed a child off a bridge once and even kicked little Anna Maria without feeling a note of remorse. Whether these accounts are true or not is disputed, but it's evident that Salvador's eccentric nature was already developing. He was flamboyant, expressive, and occasionally a rebellious and difficult pupil to boot.

As the spoiled Salvador was growing into an artist, Europe had dissolved into chaos. The First World War raged on, but it had little effect on Salvador's life. His family was well off and safe in Figueres; Salvador was lucky to be too young to fight, and he may have been barely aware of the war itself, as he was much too busy with art to concern himself with battles or politics—a stance that he would maintain for the rest of his life. Salvador was sheltered from the war just as he had been sheltered from every kind of hardship.

There was one thing, though, that even the doting Felipa could not protect Salvador from no matter how much she must have wanted to—her death.

Chapter 3 – Growing Wings

Felipa had always loved making beautiful things. This was a trait she had inherited from her own mother, Maria Anna. The specialty of the latter was paper cut-outs. She loved to cut out intricate forms to entertain her grandchildren, and for Felipa, entertaining the children would become a motivation for her own art, too. She loved to design all manners of beautiful little household objects and had been given the opportunity and materials to express herself thanks to the fact that her mother owned and worked in a haberdashery workshop. Felipa's father, Anselm, had died when she was only thirteen years old.

Felipa was 26 when she married Salvador Dalí the elder, having met him on holiday in Cabrils. Thanks to his position as the *notario* of Figueres, Salvador Senior was well-off enough that Felipa could stay at home with her children. She still indulged in her artistic nature, even though art would never become her career. Small, beautiful things populated the home as the young Salvador grew up, and he and his mother shared a love of beauty and art that drew them ever closer. He was particularly enchanted by the colorful candles that his mother loved to make, as she would often mold them into the figures of lovely things that drew Salvador's attention and made him want to make pretty things too.

Indulgent though she may have been, Felipa was undoubtedly deeply loving, and she supported her son and doted on him in every way that she knew how. She became his staunchest friend and advocate, his rock, and his biggest fan. Salvador would later describe his relationship with her as something akin to worship, saying that he counted on her to "make invisible the unavoidable blemishes of [his] soul." She was everything to him.

And in 1921, she died.

It was uterine cancer. Modern medicine could have saved baby Salvador from gastroenteritis, but even today, the cancer that spread swiftly through Felipa's body would likely have been a death sentence. Salvador was a happy, carefree, confident, young artist one moment, on the fast track to becoming another of Spain's greats. The next, he was robbed of the person he loved the most in the entire world. He was only seventeen, and his delicate young mind had not yet been exposed to true loss. The death of his mother was the first crushing blow he would experience, and it was a terrible one. He was unable to accept the fact that Felipa was gone. "I could not resign myself to the loss of [my mother]," he wrote in his autobiography.

Stone-hearted Salvador Senior may not have felt the same. He appears to have loved Felipa, but he replaced her swiftly. In 1922, he remarried—and his new wife was Felipa's younger sister, Catalina. Salvador's aunt abruptly became his stepmother. One can imagine that this might have caused significant tension between Salvador and his father, but young Salvador appears to have had a happy relationship with Catalina, his much-loved aunt. Perhaps she reminded both Salvadors of the sweet and wonderful woman that they had lost.

The loss of Felipa was something that would never let go of Salvador. His grief never left him, and the rest of his life, as well as his art, would always be affected by the fact that she was gone. Grief, however, failed to staunch the flow of creativity from Salvador's developing mind. Despite the loss of his greatest supporter, Salvador became more determined than ever to achieve greatness in his art. "I had to achieve glory," he wrote, "to avenge the affront caused to me by the death of my mother who I adored." He threw himself into his art with even greater passion.

Before the death of his mother, Salvador had taken to painting some of his first portraits. Ironically, one of his first portraits was not of his beloved and doting mother. Instead, it was of his father. *The Artist's Father at Llane Beach and View of Portdogue* (1920) depicts Salvador Senior standing by the beach. His face is turned away from the viewer, and there is something pensive in the furrow of his brows, yet it's easy to see from the stern lines of his nose and mouth that Salvador Senior was not lenient. From 1920 to 1921, Salvador painted *The Vegetable Garden of Llaner*, a peaceful scene of a vegetable garden. This was likely Salvador's last painting before the death of his mother.

His next painting was *Cabaret Scene* (1922), and the difference between this and his previous paintings is utterly striking. That year had been a tumultuous one for Salvador. Not only had his father married Catalina, but he had also begun to express his distaste for Salvador's chosen career path. Felipa had been the one who had always supported young Salvador; now, Salvador Senior had changed his mind, deciding that he was no longer content with allowing the boy to study art. He wanted him to instead become a professor. Salvador railed heartily against his father's change of heart, and the two eventually came to an agreement: Salvador could study art, but he had to do it at the Royal Academy of Fine Arts in Madrid, where he could attain the title of a professor.

So, Salvador found himself being packed off alone across the country, leaving behind the snow-capped mountaintops and lush green fields and quiet gardens of Figueres to find his feet in the smoggy bustle of 1920s Madrid. The palette of his world changed abruptly. He had known green hills and blue water and pink skies; now, he knew gray streets and black suits, and this is reflected in *Cabaret Scene*. School had introduced Salvador to Cubism, the art of which Picasso was the great master, and he experimented with this style, as well as with hues of black, white, and gray. Compared with the vibrancy of *The Vegetable Garden of Llaner, Cabaret Scene* is colorless, flat, and scrambled. Perhaps Salvador's heart felt the same now that it had been stripped of its greatest love.

Madrid had also brought a sea of new people for Salvador to meet, and despite his many eccentricities, he made short work of becoming friends with a group of young artists like himself. One of these was Carles Fages de Climent, for whom Salvador created his first professional artwork, illustrations for Climent's book, *The Witches of Llers*. These drawings were wild and dark, and they remain relatively little-known. Instead, it was Salvador's love of Cubism that drew attention from his schoolmates, as well as his many, many quirks.

Free from the oppressive grip of his father's stifling hand upon him, Salvador began to explore more of his eccentricities, and his flamboyant nature began to develop—and it was on full display to all those around him thanks to his personal style. In a time when short, neat hair was in fashion for men, Salvador grew his dark locks long and added a pair of extravagant sideburns. He dressed like a gentleman of the previous century with britches and long coats that drew attention wherever he went. And although many of his schoolmates were derisive toward him, labeling him a "dandy," Salvador didn't find it hard to make friends. His most notorious friendship at this school was with Federico García Lorca.

Federico would become almost as famous as Salvador; in fact, it's rumored that Federico was the only person who was ever capable of inspiring jealousy in the heart of Salvador Dalí. Even at school, Federico was a truly brilliant poet, already publishing a volume of poetry while he was still studying. He and Salvador were both part of the famed "Generation of '27," a group of Spanish avant-garde artists of the time. It was likely their mutual love of avant-garde art that first sparked the friendship between Federico and Salvador. They grew close during their time in Madrid, but just how close is much disputed. Federico was openly homosexual, and Salvador would later claim that the young poet had made numerous sexual advances on him. According to Salvador, he had rejected them all, yet correspondence between the two young men would suggest otherwise.

Federico and Salvador certainly had much in common, and one of those things was that they would both become Surrealists during their time in Madrid.

Surrealism itself was still in its infancy in the early 1920s. The term was first used in 1917; fittingly enough, it was used to describe the ballet *Parade*, which was costumed by Pablo Picasso in characteristically imaginative fashion. Ultimately, though, this short-lived and dramatic movement was born in the mind of André Breton. Only six years older than Salvador, Breton was a Frenchman who had once been destined to become a doctor. He moved to Paris from his hometown of Tinchebray around the same time Salvador went to Madrid, and there, Breton discovered his love of avant-garde art. Breton would be more than just a member of the Generation of '27, though. He would become the pioneer of a movement that spanned all the way from art to psychology to politics.

Art that broke the rules of the norm attracted Breton because of his difficult childhood. Like Salvador, he had one atheist parent and one who was profoundly religious, but unlike the meekly devout Felipa, Breton's mother was a cold-hearted, iron-fisted ruler of the household who dished out discipline with icy rage. Breton's artistic young soul was crushed into the mold his mother demanded, and he rebelled furiously against it. In Paris, he took that rebellion even further. Breton was not interested in morality or religion or reason. He was interested in expressing himself, fully and purely, and for that reason, he wrote the Manifesto of Surrealism in 1924. The manifesto sang the praises of the subconscious mind, calling upon others to rise above and break the shackles of mere rationality and allow the mind to express itself without limits. Breton saw reason as oppressive and Surrealism as the liberation not only of art but also of all human thinking. Surrealism is known today as an art movement, but in reality, it was much more than that. If Breton would have had his way, it would have become a global revolution. Those who joined the ranks of Surrealism were expected to fully align with all of Breton's ideas—ideas that included not only art but also politics, morality, and humanity.

Surrealism encompassed filmmakers, artists, and writers, and Federico and Salvador were both fascinated by Breton's organization, although Salvador would not rush to join it. Dadaism, a similar avant-garde art movement that focused on the ideas of chance and meaninglessness, also caught Salvador's attention. He played with Dadaist art for a while, but Surrealism was ultimately what truly stuck.

Education and Surrealism together refined and developed Salvador's art and style to a great extent. School taught him more about classical art techniques, while Surrealism taught him new ways and methods that were just developing. The most popular among these was automatism, the practice of freeing the subconscious mind by making art in a stream-of-consciousness manner.

By 1925, Salvador had been studying for three years, and he was just one year away from graduating as an art professor at Madrid. He was also ready for his first solo exhibition, which he held in November 1925 at the Galeries Dalmau in Barcelona. He was not yet fully committed to Surrealism, and many of his paintings hearkened all the way back to the landscapes he had made as a child; Cadaques Bay and other landscapes, as well as his father and Anna Maria, were all featured in his paintings. *Young Woman at a Window* is a particularly poignant and gentle depiction of Anna Maria. He also painted one of his earliest self-portraits around this time, which was dedicated to Federico. Other pieces of his art were much more experimental. *Venus and Sailor* is faintly Cubist in its geometric execution; *Still Life* is another very abstract work, as is *Pierrot Playing the Guitar*. It's little wonder that critics left the exhibition puzzled as to what this young artist truly wanted to achieve; however, they were inspired by his excellent work. Salvador was very much still experimenting with styles, trying to find his niche in the art world. It would be a few more years before he truly fell in love with Surrealism and brought it into his art; for now, the public had to watch and wait.

Salvador's time at the Royal Academy of Fine Arts was coming to a close. He spent the next summer at his old haunt of Cadaques, painting his sister, the landscape, and Federico, who came with him. Salvador continued to paint various styles in 1926, from the beautifully photorealistic *The Basket of Bread* to *Cubist Figure* to the striking *Honey is Sweeter than Blood*, one of his earliest recognizably Surrealist paintings.

Salvador had seldom been as prolific, and never as sure of what he was striving to create, as when he returned to Madrid in 1926. He would not be there for very long, however. Larger than life—and at almost five feet, eight inches in a post-WWI world, Salvador was physically tall, too—and wildly eccentric, his personality was growing out of the confining walls of the Royal Academy of Fine Arts. Salvador had sprouted wings. And the young artist was about to truly take flight.

Chapter 4 – Rebellion

Salvador never did become a professor like his father wanted him to. In fact, in the next few years, he would do many things that his father didn't want him to—and being expelled from the Royal Academy of Fine Arts was just the beginning.

The academic year of 1925-26 was a lackadaisical one for Salvador Dalí; his attendance was poor, yet it was clear that he had mastered all that the school had taught him. *The Basket of Bread* demonstrated excellent technique, and even though he didn't study as hard as he probably should have, Salvador made it all the way to his very last final examination. If he had taken the exam, his natural brilliance would likely have made it an easy pass. Unfortunately, Salvador never did take it. Instead, he caused trouble, insulting his professors right before the final oral examination. Flamboyant and arrogant as he was then, Salvador thought nothing of stepping on his professors' toes, already believing himself to be a genius and far superior to most other mere mortals.

"I am infinitely more intelligent than these three professors," Salvador is said to have stated indignantly. "I therefore refuse to be examined by them. I know this subject much too well."

As one can imagine, this did not go down well with the professors, and Salvador was expelled before he could write his final. Salvador

Senior's dream of seeing his son as an art professor was crushed forever.

Free of the constraints of the lecture hall, Salvador decided to travel to the arts center of Europe: Paris. Over the next three years, he would make several trips to the City of Lights, and on one of them, he finally met the man who had been inspiring him for many years—Pablo Picasso. In fact, Picasso was the first thing he wanted to see when he arrived in Paris, even before the Louvre. Salvador had been an admirer of Picasso's ever since he was a boy, and the great Cubist himself had developed from the heartbroken youngster of the Blue Period into one of the most influential artists of his time. Himself now a Surrealist, Picasso had passed from his Blue and Rose Periods to splendid maturity. Salvador was awed to meet him, and even after parting from his first meeting with Picasso, he would continue to send letter after letter to his idol for the rest of his life—even though his worship of Picasso eventually turned into a rivalry.

Salvador might have left art school behind, but he would never abandon art itself. He continued to paint constantly, his style still very much evolving. Still, many of his paintings during this time would start to look recognizably like the style he would come to be known for. Even Dalí himself was starting to look more like the man whose face the world came to know, as it was shortly after leaving the Royal Academy of Fine Arts that he grew his characteristic pointy mustache.

Surrealist Composition (1928) was one of his first paintings to use hyper-realism fused with the uniquely dreamlike, almost hallucinogenic quality that would later become the artist's famous style; others include *Little Cinders* (1928), *Portrait of Paul Eluard* (1929), *Phantasmagoria* (c. 1929), *The Lugubrious Game* (1929), and *The Invisible Man* (c, 1929-32).

1929 was undoubtedly the year when Salvador Dalí's style truly came into its own. It was in this year that two of his most famous paintings were created, *The Great Masturbator* and *The Enigma of Desire*. While *The Enigma of Desire* was evidence of the way that Salvador's heart continued to hearken back to his mother, with the words "my mother" written in French across several parts of the painting, many of his paintings were deeply sexual in nature. This intensified throughout the year, which may be attested to the fact that 1929 was the year that Salvador met the love of his life and the muse who would continue to inspire him for the rest of his creative career: Elena Ivanovna Diakonova, better known simply as Gala.

Salvador Dalí was not the first artist that the Russian-born Gala would love. First coming to Europe in 1912 to recover in a Switzerland sanatorium from a bout of tuberculosis, Gala was eighteen years old when she met a soft-eyed Frenchman named Eugène Grindel, better known under his pen name of Paul Éluard. Éluard was a poet and one of the founders of Surrealism alongside André Breton—but all that would come later. For now, he was just a young poet hopelessly in love with a beautiful Russian girl, and before they parted ways in 1914, he proposed to her. She accepted, and they waited for three long, war-torn years (with Éluard on the front lines) before getting married in 1917.

Their marriage was a short one that was riddled with trouble. Gala met Max Ernst, a Dadaist and Surrealist pioneer, in 1922. She was still married to Éluard, but Ernst became her lover and featured her in many of his paintings. Yet Ernst was not genius enough for Gala. She would become arguably the women to be most often featured in Surrealist art after she met Salvador Dalí in 1929.

Thanks to Gala's association with both Éluard and Ernst, who were Surrealist founders, it was inevitable that she would eventually meet Salvador. He'd come to Paris for the presentation of *The Andalusian Dog*, a Surrealist film for which he'd written most of the script. The strange, silent film featured a woman's eyeball being cut in half, which was not an easy feat to pull off with 1920s special effects. A gallery owner there introduced Salvador to Paul Éluard, whom Salvador would later paint as one of his first truly Surrealist portraits, and so, inevitably, Salvador met Gala.

The moment he laid eyes on her, Salvador was enraptured by her beauty. She was ten years his senior, but there was something about her that instantly captured the young artist's hitherto unclaimed heart. Ostensibly seeking to cultivate his friendship with Éluard, Salvador invited Gala and her husband to spend some time with him at his much-loved old haunt of Cadaques, and it was on those beloved shores that their romance began to grow. Unsatisfied by either Ernst or Éluard, Gala found herself drawn in by Salvador's brilliance, quirky though he was. And although she would never find it in herself to be truly faithful to a single man, Salvador would become the one great mainstay of Gala's love life.

Their love was passionate and fierce, hot enough to quickly burn through the fading ties of Gala's marriage to Éluard. She had not left him for Ernst, but she left him quickly for Salvador, following the younger artist to Paris and divorcing Éluard once there. Not only did she leave her first husband behind, but she also practically abandoned her eleven-year-old daughter by Éluard, Cecile. From that moment on, the little girl didn't have a mother, as Gala showed no interest in her.

Salvador was elated to live with the love of his life. He would later write that the moment he laid eyes on Gala, he knew that she was "destined to become [...] the one who moves me forward, my victory, my wife." And though they were not yet married, Gala certainly proved to be a most effective muse for him.

The same year that he met Gala, Salvador officially joined the Surrealists. Gala served to be not only his muse but also his compass; in her company, he was able to see the direction in which he wanted to take his art, and he threw himself wholeheartedly into Surrealism, quickly becoming one of its greatest masters.

Salvador had never been so successful as an artist, but while his professional life was taking off, his family life had taken a sharp turn for the worse. Salvador Senior had never gotten along well with his son; his disciplinarian ways could not have been more disagreeable to Salvador's free-spirited and eccentric temperament. Even now that Salvador was 25, Salvador Senior was determined to impose his will upon the young man. Being expelled from the Royal Academy of

Fine Arts was the first blow that caused cracks to spread out across the crumbling foundation of their relationship.

The second came when Salvador exhibited a piece of art on which was written, "Sometimes I spit on the portrait of my mother for the fun of it." Salvador Senior had never gotten along with his son, but he had loved Felipa despite his speedy replacement of her, and he was shocked by Salvador's words. To make matters worse, Salvador openly started living with Gala. The pair became inseparable, and by the December holidays of 1929, it was clear to Salvador Senior that his son's relationship with the promiscuous Russian was more than just a fling. He demanded that Salvador break things off with Gala, and of course, Salvador refused. How could he abandon his muse, the love of his life?

Salvador Senior's reaction was outrage. Salvador had been spending the Christmas holidays in the family home back in Figueres with his father and Anna Maria; the house there was still more or less his home base, the place he returned to whenever he needed refuge. It would be so no more. Salvador Senior forcibly threw him out on December 28th, 1929, ordering him never to return. He was also disinherited and even told that he would never be allowed at Cadaques again.

Cadaques had, for so long, been the seat of Salvador's inspiration, yet he returned to Paris hurt but not defeated. The beautiful bays and gorgeous landscapes had been the setting for some of the happiest times of his childhood. It was at Cadaques that Salvador had first met Ramon Pichot and been introduced to the idea of modern art. Cadaques had also been depicted in so many of his first paintings. Yet Salvador no longer needed the beautiful place to be his muse. He had Gala for that instead, and when the pair moved to a home in Paris, Salvador's career truly took flight.

The early 1930s saw him paint some of his most famous masterpieces, in large part thanks to his famed paranoiac-critical method, which was to become a significant part of Surrealism. Automatism was the practice of creating art in a stream of consciousness manner without constraints. The paranoiac-critical method took this one step further. It was not merely an artistic technique; instead, it was a Surrealist manner of perceiving reality. Salvador developed this method almost single-handedly during the early 1930s. He would use psychological techniques—like others, he had been inspired by the work of Sigmund Freud—to inspire in himself a state of paranoia. Letting go of his conscious reasoning and perception of reality, he would allow himself to slip into an almost hallucinatory state until everything appeared to be warped. The resultant dreamlike trance he entered brought him some of his most famous images, and whatever he saw in his dreams, he put down upon the canvas.

Hard though it may seem to believe, at no point in Salvador's life were drugs or any other artificial hallucinogens part of his artistic process. In fact, there is no evidence to suggest that Salvador Dalí used drugs at all, either for recreation or for art. "I don't do drugs," Salvador stated. "I *am* drugs." The paranoiac-critical method proved so effective in inducing a hallucinatory state that Salvador never needed any chemical help.

The paranoiac-critical method launched his art into a new realm, defining a style that would become legendary. His 1930 paintings employ some of his typical techniques, such as hiding the figure of a face or human body in landscapes or animals; *Paranoiac Woman-Horse* is a prime example. *The Hand: Remorse of Conscience* is also a typical Dalí painting—or, as he would describe it, a "hand-painted ream photograph." This was Salvador's first depiction of Gala's face, gazing up at the sky; he painted himself with a gigantic hand stretched out over a desert landscape, preventing the dark clouds from showering the sand with rain. *The Hand* is perhaps not so much about Gala as it is about Salvador Senior. The younger Salvador would not reconcile with his father for many more years; although the rain clouds perhaps signify his desire to return to his family home, he stubbornly refused, looking to Gala as his new family instead. In 1930, the Surrealists also published Salvador's book, *The Visible Woman*, in which featured a compilation of many of his previous paintings.

The next year would see Salvador go from promising young artist to undeniable Surrealist master, for it was in 1931 that he would paint his single most famous piece, *The Persistence of Memory*.

Chapter 5 - Risen Star

Illustration II: The Temptation of Saint Anthony, *an example of one of Dalí's later works, showing the classic dreamlike quality for which he would soon be famous*

As Salvador continued to paint his dreamlike images despite the rejection he'd just suffered from his father, Spain itself was embroiled in a growing turmoil, not unlike the conflict that had erupted within the Dalí family. For eight years—from 1923 to 1931—the Spanish people had been governed ostensibly by a monarchy; however, the real ruler was General Miguel Primo de Rivera. Rivera had the monarchy under his control and effectively ruled as a dictator who did as he pleased.

1929, however, brought the Wall Street Crash with it, sending ripples of economic disaster all over the globe. Europe had barely recovered from the First World War and was steadily tottering toward the Second World War, and international trade relations had never been so fraught. The Spanish economy plummeted alongside the rest of the world, and its people became more and more dissatisfied. Eventually, Rivera and King Alfonso XIII were forced into exile in 1931, and so began the Second Republic of Spain.

The Second Republic was a kind of fool's gold for the Spanish people. They believed that their troubles were over, that the Second Republic would rebuild their country into the mighty and prosperous power that it once had been. Salvador was experiencing a similar hope as he grew into his new life with Gala. She inspired him so greatly that, in 1931, he signed his first painting as *Gala-Dalí* in blood red. In typical dramatic fashion, he explained this by saying that he painted mostly with her blood. The painting, *They Were There*, was unusual for Salvador in that it was actually quite ordinary: a fairly straightforward portrait of an unknown man looking directly at the viewer, with very little Surrealist qualities.

That is not to say that Salvador had given up on Surrealism. Indeed, he painted more Surrealist images in 1931 than in any of the preceding years. Ghosts, desert landscapes, shadows, and seashells were prominent images; the paintings were also more contemplative in this year than in the years before, although a few erotic sketches were created. There is also a fabulously beautiful, vibrant, even joyous portrait of Gala in the brightest colors.

But it was not the portrait that would make Salvador famous. Instead, it was *The Persistence of Memory*.

It doesn't take an art connoisseur to recognize Salvador Dalí's most famous painting. Melting clocks draped over the Catalonian landscape have practically become the face of Surrealism itself. It features numerous pocket watches, some of them melting, with one being destroyed by ants. Even though Salvador's father had banned him from ever visiting Cadaques again, the beautiful bay was still a part of him, and he incorporated it into his painting—Mount Panié's shadow falls across the front of the painting, and the Cap de Creus peninsula is visible in the background. A strange, molten profile in the middle of the painting is almost exactly the same as the central shape in *The Great Masturbator*, which was likely a self-portrait.

The painting is the glorious marriage of all the things that made Salvador unique: his realism, his paranoiac-critical method, his love of Freudian theories, and—according to Salvador himself—the observation of a wheel of Camembert cheese melting in the sun. Some postulate that Einstein's theory of relativity inspired part of the painting, too, in that the clocks slowly oozing into liquid signify the relationship between space and time. This would not be the first time that science inspired Dalí's art.

To the Surrealists, *The Persistence of Memory* was a triumph, a pinnacle of their movement. And to Salvador, it was an undeniable masterpiece. It was well-received in Europe, but it wasn't in Europe that the painting made Salvador Dalí a household name. Instead, it would be all the way across the ocean. Salvador had outgrown Europe. He was about to be introduced to the city that never sleeps.

Salvador himself would not journey to New York until 1934, but *The Persistence of Memory* was shipped across the sea to the United States two years earlier in 1932. There, art dealer Julien Levy had organized a Surrealist exhibition, one of the first to reach the US. Harvard-educated Levy had been fascinated by the modern art movement for years, first coming across Dadaism in an early 1920s trip to Paris, then naturally becoming interested in Surrealism. He was a particularly vociferous advocate of photography, which was not yet considered art in those days, and when he inherited money from his deceased mother, Levy was able to open his own gallery around 1931. He strove to exhibit fine photography and convince the New York art fraternity that pictures were just as valuable as paintings.

In 1932, Levy held his first Surrealist exhibition at his gallery, and masterpieces from numerous artists were brought to New York from Europe for the show. Max Ernst was among them; Gala's erstwhile lover sent several pieces to New York, where they were shown amongst Salvador's. One of the paintings that Salvador elected to send to New York, not yet knowing that it would become utterly iconic, was *The Persistence of Memory*. From the moment the gallery doors opened, the painting of the soft watches seized the attention of art enthusiasts all over the city. Its intriguing composition was just as remarkable then as it is now, and people flocked to see the melting clocks. The painting was an instant hit, and almost overnight, Salvador Dalí was famous. Ernst's dark and chaotic scenes couldn't hope to compare with Salvador's.

In the meantime, Salvador and Gala had purchased their first home together in Port Lligat. It was just a cabin, which they had originally rented. However, the early 1930s were financially kind to Salvador, and with Gala astutely managing his business affairs, he was soon able to buy his cabin and then the neighboring properties, too. Salvador gradually grew the humble little home into a large and extravagant villa.

Gala had not only become his lover; in some ways, she had replaced the late Felipa in the role of Salvador's life manager. The artist was brilliant, intelligent, and hardworking; he was not, however, practical. It would be difficult to expect someone who had openly disavowed reality and reason to be able to manage his money and business correctly. That role fell to Gala, and she was both manager and muse. She must have been adept at both because Salvador was painting more than ever before. As before, Catalonia, bread, strange dreamlike objects, sex, and the words "my mother" were constant themes of Salvador's art. There was also another breathtaking portrait of Gala. Perhaps best known of his 1932-33 paintings is *The Invisible Man* (1932), in which a male figure is hidden in a chaotic landscape.

By 1934, *The Persistence of Memory* had made Salvador famous, at least in New York, but Americans had still never seen Salvador in the flesh. The man who would seek to remedy that fact was Pablo Picasso. Salvador's idol worship of Picasso had never ended. He continued to write endless letters to the great Cubist master, and Picasso was seeing real potential in him, potential far beyond what he had expected upon meeting the enthusiastic but directionless young painter six years before. Now Salvador was thirty years old; he was sure of his style, had created three of his most famous paintings, and had become an icon of Surrealism. Suitably impressed, Picasso approached Salvador to tell him that he needed to go to New York—and that Picasso himself would pay for his and Gala's passage to the United States.

New York was whipped into a frenzy when the people heard that Salvador Dalí, the man with the melting clocks, was coming to town. *The Persistence of Memory* had been a sensation, and reports had reached the city that its creator was just as unique as the iconic painting. When Salvador and Gala arrived on a steamboat from Europe, the New York crowds that had gathered to see the great Surrealist were not disappointed. Salvador's pointy mustache and larger-than-life demeanor were an instant hit with Americans. His signature move was to strut out of his hotel on East 55th Street and call out, "Dalí is here!" to raucous cheers from his audience.

It was in the room of that same hotel that *Time* magazine first encountered Salvador Dalí, and the illustrious publication's reporters were instantly given an impression of the Surrealist master's personality when they stepped into his room. He had transformed his own hotel room into a Surrealist composition: the table lamp was balanced on the rocking chair, which, in turn, was balanced on the table alongside a Catalan liberty cap in red plush.

He was a showman in every fiber of his body, and he lapped up every drop of adoration and glee from the crowds. They loved him, and Salvador's already swollen ego was bolstered by their constant adoration. He was free at last, and the more avant-garde he was, the more New York loved him. It must have felt to Salvador as if he had finally found his artistic home, thousands of miles from the place where he'd grown up. Figueres had been a small town, Cadaques, a soothing retreat, and Madrid, a learning curve. And while Paris might have been the arts and culture capital of Europe, there was still something much too classical about it for Salvador's taste. New York was the place to be, he realized. And although the city was a very long way from his house in Spain, it would, in many ways, become his home.

New York adored him so much that members of high society there decided that it would be a good idea to throw a special ball in honor of nobody but Salvador Dalí. He was absolutely delighted by the idea of an entire ball being dedicated to him, and he knew he needed to give the crowd that came to see him a suitable show. When Dalí arrived at the ball, he was wearing a costume of his own design—a glass case affixed to his chest, containing a bra. Gala does not appear to have been even remotely phased by her husband's eccentric dress code.

Perhaps because of his prominent use of lingerie in his costume, Caresse Crosby, who had invented the bra in the first place, invited Salvador and Gala to a costumed ball at her house. There, Salvador made one of the very few choices for which he would later apologize: he and Gala dressed as Charles Lindbergh Jr. and his kidnapper. At the time, the case of the kidnapped Lindbergh baby was still under investigation, and the tale is a tragic one indeed. Famous aviator Charles Lindbergh's infant son had been kidnapped in 1932, and years of negotiations followed, including a $50,000 ransom (almost a million dollars in today's money) being paid to the kidnapper, who simply called himself "John." The baby was never returned after the ransom was paid, and his decomposed body was later found half-buried in a field. The poor child had been killed by a blow to the head. Gala and Salvador's costumes understandably sparked outrage, and despite protestations from the Surrealists (who believed that apologies, like morality, were nothing but a constraint upon the human mind), Salvador apologized publicly for his choice of outfit.

Apologizing for dressing like a murdered baby was not the only thing Salvador did that was frowned upon by the Surrealists. Upon his return to Europe in 1934, Salvador discovered that he was in hot water with the organization of which he'd become one of the most famous members. And this time, it was for his politics.

As much as Salvador claimed that his art, as well as his life, was apolitical, there were signs that he sympathized with one of history's most terrifying and horrific figures: Adolf Hitler. He would later admit that he had erotic dreams about Hitler (saying that he often dreamed of Hitler "as other men would dream about women"), and a fascination with the Nazi leader was evident in his art, with three paintings explicitly named after him created from 1939 onward. André Breton and most of the other prominent Surrealists were communists, clinging desperately to their ideals. Fascism was on the rise; Hitler was in control of Germany, Spain was rapidly heading that way itself, and tension between fascists and other ideologies was intensifying—and it would continue to intensify into the global disaster that was the Second World War. Unlike Breton and others, Salvador was not blatantly communist. There was no neutrality in those years just before WWII. One could be either friend or foe, and as Salvador would not identify himself as friend, Breton and the others decided he had to be an enemy.

When Salvador returned from New York, the Surrealists held a "trial" for him in order to decide whether or not he was fit to remain within the organization. Despite the fact that Salvador protested that he was not a fascist and that his fascination with Hitler was on a subconscious Surrealist level, he was promptly expelled from the group. And while Salvador never actively supported any fascist cause, it is difficult to say that he was not actually a fascist. General Francisco Franco, the Spanish dictator who would rise to power after the Spanish Civil War, was as fascist as they come, and Salvador hailed him as a hero. In some ways, it's possible that Salvador Senior was right. Surrealism really had eaten away at Salvador's morals.

Being expelled from Surrealism failed to perturb Salvador much. His boundless confidence was hardly affected at all by his expulsion from Breton's organization; they couldn't stop him from making Surrealist art or being the most famous Surrealist painter in history, so he wasn't particularly bothered. His words regarding his "excommunication" from Surrealism were succinct, arrogant in the extreme, and quintessentially Dalí.

"The difference between the Surrealists and me," he said, "is, I myself am Surrealism." Egocentric as this statement may sound, Salvador was not exactly wrong; decades after Surrealism died with André Breton, it is not Breton's work that is most recognizable as Surrealist in the modern day but Salvador Dalí's.

1934 was a great year for the thirty-year-old artist. As well as his trip to New York, he also took the plunge and married Gala after five years of living with her. No church was involved; instead, the ceremony was purely civil. And Salvador Senior, who had thrown his son out of the house half a decade ago, did not come to the wedding.

Chapter 6 – Fame and Eccentricity

When Salvador Dalí entered the lecture hall dressed in an old diving suit, nobody was surprised.

It was the London International Surrealist Exhibition of 1936, after all. No one actually expected Salvador Dalí, of all people, to deliver his much-anticipated lecture looking even remotely normal. The exhibition itself had been fairly chaotic already; organized by two young British Surrealists, it aimed to bring the movement to England, where it hadn't really caught on yet. The exhibition itself had almost been doomed from the start. The Brits, not possessing the more lenient outlook of the French and Spanish, were not amused with many of the sexually charged Surrealist drawings and confiscated some of them at customs because of their indecency. Once the organizers of the exhibition—Roland Penrose and David Gascoyne—had succeeded in getting the paintings back and hanging them in the Burlington Gallery, a collector named E. L. T. Mesens decided that the arrangement was much too ordinary and sowed utter chaos by switching all the paintings around. Salvador, for his part, had ensured that the exhibition started off with a bang. He dressed fellow Surrealist and actress Sheila Legge in a white gown and covered her face with a garland, then equipped her with a raw pork chop and an artificial limb before sending her off to walk around Trafalgar Square. (Incidentally, this was not the first time that Salvador had used a pork chop as a strange kind of sexual symbol; he had painted Gala with lamb chops on her shoulders in 1933.) The raw pork chop was a regrettable decision and briskly began to smell appalling, and Legge fled back into the gallery, but Salvador's plan had certainly worked. Londoners could not help but take notice.

Now, a group of Surrealist enthusiasts and other interested parties waited with bated breath for the famed Salvador Dalí to deliver his lecture on Surrealism. Surely, they thought, no one understood it better than the master himself. He certainly looked the part as he squeaked and creaked his way into the lecture hall dressed head to toe for diving, from the long suit to the gigantic diving helmet. He also carried a billiard cue in one hand; in the other, he held the leashes of two enormous dogs. They were graceful creatures yet undeniably odd-looking, with long, curly coats, bulbous eyes, and Roman noses, pacing effortlessly into the room on deer-like legs. These uniquely beautiful Borzois originated from Russia—possibly a nod to Gala's origins.

Salvador handed over the cue and the Borzois and began to deliver his lecture. Unfortunately, it is doubtful whether anyone actually heard a word of it. To start with, Salvador's voice was badly muffled by the diving helmet, reducing it to a mere echoing gong sound somewhere deep inside the thick glass. His lecture was accompanied with slides, but Salvador had elected to display all of them upside down. To make matters worse, somewhere around the middle of his lecture, Salvador began to suffocate inside his diving helmet. His audience believed this was all part of the show and watched pleasurably as Salvador began to stagger around, clutching at his throat and vainly attempting to pull off the helmet; only Gascoyne had the presence of mind to find a spanner and loosen the helmet as Salvador crumpled to the floor. The audience, awed, watched as Gascoyne pulled the helmet off to reveal a red-faced and panting Salvador, his iconic mustache slightly askew.

Salvador was somewhat asphyxiated, but he was nonetheless unperturbed. "I was trying to show that I was plunging deep into the human mind," he said. It's still unclear exactly what the contents of his lecture turned out to be, but the Surrealist master had gotten his point across as only he could.

The exhibition, held in 1936, proved to be a roaring success despite the relative lack of Surrealism in Britain prior to the exhibition. More than thirty thousand people came to see this new style of art. Salvador's fame continued to grow, and he was constantly painting throughout this time. He produced one of his most famous works that year, *Lobster Telephone*. This was not a painting but rather a Surrealist object. Vaguely menacing and frankly weird, *Lobster Telephone* is exactly what it sounds like—an early telephone with a lobster spread across the mouthpiece. This was not the first time that Salvador had used a lobster in his artwork; he had often used these innocent sea creatures to cover the crotches of his female nudes in paintings. In fact, Salvador produced more than sixty works of art in 1936, making it one of his most prolific years. *Soft Construction with Boiled Beans* was another well-known piece, a typical Dalí painting with melting human figures merging into one another.

He subtitled the latter painting *Premonition of Civil War*, and civil war was about to erupt indeed.

Spain's Second Republic started out as a beacon of hope, but it quickly turned out to be little more than a mirage. Only five years after the Second Republic began, it crumbled hideously. General Francisco Franco, a career soldier and loyal monarchist, had been slowly inching his way up the ladder in the conservative party ever since crushing the October Revolution of 1933. Even though the liberals had maintained control over the Second Republic, and Franco had been practically banished to an outlying garrison in Morocco after dealing with the revolution, the conservatives were still quietly gaining power. Communism was growing in popularity as the Soviet Union started to flex its considerable muscles, and the liberals were leaning more and more to the left. Franco was no fan of Marx. Neither, however, did he believe in freedom. Instead, Franco was as fascist as they come, and he was determined to impose his rigid beliefs on the people of Spain.

In 1936, as the Republic leaned ever more toward communism, Franco made his move. The conservative group had been pressuring him to work with them for some time, and he finally gave in during the summer of 1936. A revolution began, with Franco leading the rebels, who were composed of members of various political parties. Collectively, they were known as the Nationalists. It started in Spanish Morocco, where it quickly gained ground. Madrid stood firm against the Nationalists, and so did Catalonia, which had been ferociously independent during the Second Republic. Franco, however, was both powerful and adept. He worked fast to overwhelm the group of parties styling themselves as the Loyalists. By November of that year, Madrid—the city where Salvador Dalí had first learned how to paint like a master—was under siege.

Salvador was not deeply affected by the outbreak of this war at first. His possible pro-fascist outlook would have dulled the edge of the fear of Franco that many other people felt; in fact, Salvador was possibly in favor of the Nationalists winning the war. It's hard to tell, however, because unlike many Surrealist artists, Salvador didn't choose a side. Most famous Spanish artists were fleeing into exile as the Nationalists gained strength. Many Surrealists were profoundly leftist, and they painted in favor of their chosen ideology. Others supported Franco. Salvador, however, openly supported no one at all. He continued to paint his strange and lovely dreams, and he lived with Gala in Catalonia, far from the trouble.

Salvador would not be unaffected by the war for long, though. In August 1936, shortly after Franco launched his first attack, one of Salvador's oldest friends fell victim to the bloody battles.

Federico García Lorca, Salvador's university friend and possible lover, had built up a prestigious Surrealist writing career. Like Salvador, he had attracted American attention and traveled to New York after publishing his poetry collection, *Gypsy Ballads*, in 1928. In 1933, he wrote his famous *Blood Wedding*, a tragic folk play often performed by his own traveling theater company. *Blood Wedding*'s themes were close to Lorca's heart, as it starred ordinary Spanish women who threw off the shackles of society's expectations and lived with passion and courage.

Outsider though he was, Lorca refused to be stopped by the fact that he was different than everyone else. Instead, he made his uniqueness his superpower. Unlike Salvador, Lorca remained close to the Surrealists and their leftist associations. And so it was that, inevitably, when the Nationalists advanced in an unstoppable wave on Granada, Lorca hurried to hide in his home. His friends defended his case when Nationalist police and army officers sought to investigate him, but it was all in vain. In August 1936, the police invaded Lorca's house, arrested him, and loaded him into a car. He was taken away forcefully, never to be seen again.

Official Spanish records state that Lorca immediately "confessed," although it's clear that no trial followed, and there's no evidence of what exactly he confessed to. A firing squad was assembled, and together with two others, Lorca was shot to death, his brilliant mind splintered into bloody gray fragments by the bullets. They threw him into a shallow ravine and left one of the great Surrealist writers of all time to rot in the Spanish sun.

Salvador's expulsion from the Surrealists likely saved him from the same fate as his old friend. There is little indication to suggest that Salvador and Lorca were still close, and Salvador continued to paint and advance his career undeterred despite the war.

This was, in large part, thanks to one of Salvador's wealthiest patrons: Sir Edward James, a British poet. Largely unaffected by the civil war in Spain, Sir Edward was able to collaborate with Salvador on some of his projects and was also able to buy them from him, including *Lobster Telephone* and *Mae West Lips Sofa* (1937).

In America, Salvador had continued to make waves in the two years since his first visit. Surrealism, which had first been considered to be a silly fad, had become an art movement in the United States. The Museum of Modern Art continued to exhibit Surrealist paintings, including Salvador's. It's not too much to say that it was Salvador's persona, as well as his art, that sparked widespread interest in Surrealism in the US. His handsome, quirky appearance, flamboyant personality, and over-the-top showmanship were irresistible to the American audience, and Surrealism itself grew in popularity as its most eccentric master grew in fame.

When *The Persistence of Memory* first came to New York in 1932, Salvador had been a nobody. By 1934, he'd gained the interest of the New York art fraternity, but by 1936, that interest had grown to include many Americans. The chaos in Spain, the chaos in Salvador's mind—it was all fascinating, and *Time* magazine knew it. The magazine, whose reporters had first walked into his hotel room back in 1934 to see it adorned by a table lamp on a rocking chair on a table, now decided that Salvador was more than a feature; he was a cover star. On December 14th, 1936, *Time* magazine published a photograph of Salvador on the cover. He was not wearing his characteristic skyward mustache in the photo, nor one of his outrageous facial expressions; instead, the photograph portrays a more serious and contemplative side of the young man, a side that mourned the loss of his relationship with his father, a side that grieved the death of Lorca.

Outrageous as his behavior continued to be, and as strange as his paintings were, Salvador was still human somewhere underneath his crazy persona. This was evidenced the most in his relationship with his father.

Ever since being disinherited and thrown out of his home in 1929, Salvador had had little contact with his father, who wanted nothing to do with him. But the intervening years had perhaps begun to change Salvador Senior's mind. As Spain slipped toward civil war, the two Salvadors' attitudes to one another began to soften. In 1935, the reconciliation took place at last. Strangely enough, it was the younger Salvador who first reached out to his father. His apparently ironclad arrogance was not impenetrable against his need to obtain Salvador Senior's forgiveness. Still, whether it was pride or fear that stopped him, he found himself unable to contact his father directly. Instead, he went to his uncle, Rafael Santos Torroella, for help. Rafael was delighted to hear that Salvador wished to contact his father, and he quickly contacted Salvador Senior to request a meeting.

Salvador Senior, however, was as rigid in his grudge as he had been in his discipline. He refused to even speak to Salvador unless the latter openly left Surrealism behind. Surrealism had made Salvador both rich and famous; Gala had also told him that he could never break off his association with the movement, threatening to leave him if he did. He pleaded with Rafael to tell Salvador Senior that he couldn't leave Surrealism, but if Salvador Senior didn't forgive him, the younger Salvador would kill himself.

Salvador's entreaties finally moved Salvador Senior's iron heart. He agreed to meet with his boy in Figueres, even if it was not to actually forgive him. Rafael and Salvador journeyed to the artist's hometown for the first time in many years and met with Salvador Senior in the home where Salvador had grown up, the home whose hallways still seemed to ring with the merry laughter of Felipa.

There, a difficult scene awaited Salvador Dalí, a scene that would have enormously shocked his admirers in New York had they witnessed it. The flamboyant man who wore diving suits to lectures, who put pork chops on women's shoulders, and who painted burning giraffes with naked women, the man who was the very face of an art movement that denounced reason and praised spontaneity and the subconscious above all else, was reduced to a sobbing wreck by the rage of his father. Salvador Senior was staunch; he would not forgive Salvador unless he left the Surrealists. His anger drove the younger Salvador literally to his knees. Tears streamed down his face, and he was suddenly and tremendously human as he begged his father to relent.

And his father did relent, eventually, after endless pleading. When Anna Maria, who had been away with her friends that morning, walked back into her home, it was to a scene that she had longed for nearly six years: the two Salvadors standing together, locked in an embrace.

In public, Salvador maintained his vibrant persona, not allowing the rest of the world any glimpses into his private life. He was still as melodramatic as ever, as much so in his rage as he was in his pride and vanity. An early example of this occurred in the showing of a film in 1936. *Rose Hobart*, an American Surrealist film, was a collage of film cut from *East of Borneo* and an eclipse documentary. The film was less than twenty minutes long, but it remains one of America's most famous Surrealist pieces. Its creator, Joseph Cornell, was utterly obsessed with actress Rose Hobart, hence the title of the piece.

It was shown in 1936 in New York at the same time as the Museum of Modern Art was exhibiting some of Salvador's work; Dalí was in the city at the time, and he, of course, attended the screening of Cornell's film. The film sparked extravagant rage in Salvador's heart. This was not because it was poor; instead, it was brilliant—much too brilliant. So brilliant that Salvador instantly had to claim it as his own. He leaped to his feet in the middle of the film and rushed upon one of the projectors, throwing it down in a rage. Lights spun crazily in the cinema as he declared furiously, "My idea for a film is exactly that! I was going to propose it to someone who would pay to have it made. I never wrote it down or told it to anyone, but it is as if he had stolen it." He stormed out of the cinema in a fury, and the anecdote became yet another sample of Dalí's eccentricity.

Salvador's popularity had increased in his own family, and it was increasing all over the world. *Time* magazine had been just the beginning. Salvador's fame would only grow as Spain tumbled deeper and deeper into madness.

Chapter 7 – The Bathtub and the Window

Illustration III: Dalí's Metamorphosis of Narcissus

In 1937, while other nations became involved in the Spanish Civil War and the fight against fascism became more and more global, Salvador Dalí painted a burning giraffe.

It was a silhouette of a giraffe, to be more precise, with flames all the way down its back and smoke curling from it. The giraffe was only part of the intricate work of art, though. Most of the canvas was filled with strange, feminine figures, propped up with Salvador's characteristic crutches, and decorated with melting clocks and covered in drawers. The drawers signified Freudian psychoanalysis as opening the human psyche for further examination. There's something dark about the painting, though. Something about the shadowy figures staggering across the landscape, the apparently calm giraffe with flames bursting across its fur, is menacing in a way that most of Dalí's paintings are not. Dalí used to say that the image of the burning giraffe was a premonition of war. If that was true, then perhaps the giraffe should have been seventy feet high with real flames erupting from its back in order to be worthy of the war that was coming.

Franco had unified the Nationalists under his iron rule, and he was driving deeper and deeper into Loyalist territory. Franco and the Nationalists had control over most of Spain's army and police force; however, there were still many Loyalist sympathizers who would gladly have taken arms against the Nationalists, if there had been arms for them to bear. The fight was growing increasingly one-sided, and the Loyalists had no choice. They turned openly to communism and called on sympathetic countries to help. The Soviet Union rushed to the aid of the Loyalists; they were countered by Italy and Germany, who were quick to support pro-fascist Franco. Thus, the Spanish Civil War, in some ways, became the first theater of World War II.

Salvador's country was being torn apart in front of his eyes, and while the artist remained relatively safe in Catalonia (which would be the last province to fall to Franco), *The Burning Giraffe* (1937) is perhaps a testimony to his growing fear. *Swans Reflecting Elephants* was another 1937 masterpiece, showing more of Salvador's use of optical illusion. It is a serenely beautiful piece, elegantly depicting nature.

That year, he also painted *The Metamorphosis of Narcissus*, his imagining of the ancient Greek myth of Narcissus. Half-nymph, half-man, Narcissus was impossibly beautiful and impossibly vain. He broke the hearts of all who yearned after his beauty, whether they were male or female, and spent his life wandering in search of something as lovely as himself. He finally found it in a pool of water: his own reflection. Falling immediately in love with himself, the young beauty starved on the bank of the pool, gazing into his own fading eyes. Salvador's painting depicts him slowly turning into the narcissus flower. He accompanied the painting with a lengthy and breathtaking poem, almost an ode to Narcissus himself, although it's easy to see why the artist identified so strongly with the man who died pining after his own reflection.

1938 was another bloody year in the raging Spanish Civil War. Franco's successes were continuing to grow, and he pushed relentlessly into the Loyalist forces, shoving his armies like a wedge into the very heart of Loyalist territory to effectively split them in half. The Loyalists were heavily compromised, and Franco began to set his sights on the proudest province of them all: Catalonia, Salvador's home.

Catalonia would put up a tremendous fight, holding Franco off for months as Salvador continued to paint and live with endless flamboyance. With Gala adeptly managing his business affairs, Salvador could continue to expand his villa and paint as he pleased. He painted *Spain*, a harsh and gruesome composition, as fragmented and desolate as his country was becoming, as well as *Apparition of Face and Fruit Dish on a Beach* and the dark and strange *Debris of an Automobile Giving Birth to a Blind Horse Biting a Telephone*, which is about as complicated as it sounds. The latter is still exhibited at the Museum of Modern Art today. He also created *Rainy Taxi*, a strange object consisting of a real car with mannequins arranged inside. One has a shark head, while another wears an evening gown and has live snails crawling across it, or at least it did when it was displayed at the International Surrealist Exhibition alongside the works of two of Salvador's rivals—Breton and Éluard.

Salvador also painted numerous well-known figures, including Abraham Lincoln, Vermeer, and himself. But most exciting of all—at least for Salvador—was a portrait he painted in a London home, a portrait of Sigmund Freud himself.

Moravian-born Freud had spent most of his life living and working in Vienna, where he had studied medicine. After graduating, he was quick to specialize in psychology, and he soon became one of history's most famous and influential thinkers on the topic. Although Freud has been thoroughly debunked numerous times, it is still clear that he was a progressive thinker and one that has had a profound effect on psychology for more than a century. His first book, *Studies in Hysteria*, was published in 1895; he would go on to produce seven more well-known volumes, the most famous of which was likely *The Interpretation of Dreams* (1900).

Freud was a pioneer in his field and discovered some of psychology's most important components. He was one of the first to interpret dreams on a psychological level, as well as the first to explore the field of psychoanalysis, a study of the unconscious with the aim of developing effective therapies for the treatment of mental illnesses. While psychoanalysis generally made people uncomfortable (most notably Einstein, who refused to let Freud analyze him), it is still relevant today. Free association, psychosexual development, and the ego were also topics introduced by Freud.

Freud's writings on the subconscious were hugely inspiring to André Breton, and they helped form the foundation of much of Surrealism. In Freud's own words, he had become the "patron saint" of Surrealism, but regrettably, the great doctor himself had little time for the movement. This was thanks to Breton's unexpected arrival at his door one day in 1921. Breton demanded attention and validation from Freud, who, bewildered, received him harshly. Breton still went on to found Surrealism based on many of Freud's concepts, but he would describe him as "an old man without elegance."

Salvador suffered none of these misgivings when it came to Freud. Back in the 1920s, he had spent much of his time wandering the streets of Vienna, trying to get up the courage to meet with his hero. Freud had been inspiring him for more than a decade, but this was the one time in which Salvador found himself trapped in shyness.

1938 was the year when Salvador finally scraped together the guts to arrange a meeting with Freud. This was probably for two reasons. The first was that Freud had been forced to flee Vienna that year, leaving behind the city where he had lived and worked for around seventy years. The Nazis had invaded Austria, and they destroyed Freud's work, burning his books, and were likely to capture and execute him next. The octogenarian had no choice but to leave his home and travel to London instead, living not very far from Salvador's friend and patron, Sir Edward James.

The other reason was that Freud was simply getting old. He was 81 already, had just suffered a terrible blow, and Salvador knew that his brilliant mind would not be so keen—or even present at all—for much longer. It was now or never. Salvador spoke to another exiled Austrian, Stefan Zweig, a poet and personal friend, asking if he would introduce him to Freud. Zweig agreed, somehow managing to persuade the grumpy old man to meet with a crazy young Spanish Surrealist.

Gala, Salvador, and Sir Edward showed up at Freud's house, and Salvador was practically trembling with anticipation. He had worshiped Freud like an idol; meeting him was almost indescribably terrifying. It wasn't just that Salvador wanted to see Freud face to face the way that a jeweler wants to see the Cullinan Diamond. He wanted something from Freud, something that can only be described as validation. The greatest ego of them all was reduced to a trembling wreck faced with his inspiration, as if he was a child holding up a crayon drawing to his father, saying, "Do you like it, Daddy?"

To that end, Salvador brought with him *The Metamorphosis of Narcissus*, tucked securely under Sir Edward's arm, for Freud's inspection. The old man received Salvador with a kind of bemused gruffness. He cracked a bad joke about Spaniards, saying that if all Spanish people looked like Salvador, it was no wonder that they were stuck in a civil war. Then, observing *The Metamorphosis*, he told Salvador that where he normally looked for the unconscious in a classical painting, he was seeking the conscious in Salvador's art. Salvador tremulously offered to sketch Freud. His sketch is filled with frantic, sweeping lines, perhaps indicative of his nervousness; the figure's eyes are pure white, hidden behind Freud's little oval glasses, perhaps showing how mysterious he appeared to Salvador.

Two less likely geniuses in a room together could hardly have been imagined. There was staid, stern Freud, a doctor, a man of science, old and exiled in his ordinary suit with a white beard; and then there was wild, famous Salvador Dalí with a pointy mustache and a Surrealist painting. It did not appear to go well, and Salvador slunk away with his tail between his legs, feeling utterly rejected by the one person whom he hoped to please. Freud, however, was anything but displeased. He would later write to Zweig, thanking him for the pleasure of meeting Salvador and adding that while he'd made up his mind that all Surrealists were frankly insane, Salvador was different. "That young Spaniard, however, with his candid and fanatical eyes, and his undeniable technical mastery, has made me reconsider my opinion."

Zweig shared Freud's words with Salvador, who was absolutely delighted by them. He particularly liked being called a fanatic. It was just in time, too, as Freud would die the following year at the age of 83, having changed the face of psychology, and of art, forever. The sketch that Salvador made of him still hangs in his London house today.

Freud was not the only celebrity that Salvador met that year. He was also invited to the home of another type of artist: fashion designer Coco Chanel. Chanel, born in France, was just as famous, and just as glamorous, as Salvador, but she lacked the doting upbringing he had. Her mother died when she was only twelve, and her father decided to place her in an orphanage. That was where she learned to sew for the first time. In 1910, when she was 27 years old, she opened her first shop. She quickly became one of Europe's most iconic and influential women. Pablo Picasso and Winston Churchill were among her friends, and her billion-dollar company today remains one of fashion's most recognizable names. It was only natural that she would invite the illustrious Salvador to meet her. Chanel was enchanting, but, of course, no one could beat Gala in Salvador's eyes. He spent much of his time at her beautiful home, La Pausa, painting art that he would exhibit in New York the following year.

1938 had been a glorious year for Salvador, but it was rapidly coming to an end, and as the months marched on, so did the feet of Franco's soldiers. As much as Salvador loved his peaceful Port Lligat villa, even he was beginning to see just how badly Europe was about to be torn apart. His feelings of fear over the war are most striking in one of his later paintings, *Soldier Take Warning* (1942). It depicts a soldier looking over his shoulder at two girls raising their skirts to show him their garters, but the girls' dark hair and the dome of light cast over them by a lamp form the striking illusion of a skull with bared teeth. The soldier's eyes are filled with fear, and the painting is composed in sickly and foreboding shades of green, black, and yellow.

But back in 1938, before he created this striking work of art, Salvador had to face the changing winds. He knew the war was coming. And it would tear him away from his beloved Catalonia for many hard years.

Chapter 8 – Flight

In January 1939, Franco achieved his aim at last. Driving across Spain, he laid siege to Barcelona, the capital of Catalonia. Clinging to its independence to its very last breath, the great province could not withstand the might of Franco, who was backed by Hitler and Mussolini. Barcelona fell, and Catalonia became the last province to collapse in the face of Franco's power and fall under the cold grip of fascism.

By April, the whole of Spain had surrendered unconditionally to Franco, utterly crushed and defeated. Salvador was not in Spain on the day of the surrender. He had traveled to New York in March to take part in the New York World's Fair and to present an individual exhibition at the gallery of his old friend Julien Levy, the man who had first brought *The Persistence of Memory* to the US. Salvador also worked for Bonwit Teller, a particularly sophisticated and upper-class fashion store, where he was in charge of designing the window displays. He'd been working there since his first trip to New York—and had been sending them designs from as early as 1929—but this year would be the first time that Bonwit Teller would be dissatisfied with his work. Salvador had designed a complicated set featuring a fur-lined bathtub, standing on what looked like glowing coals, with a nude mannequin stepping seductively into it. It was certainly very different, and in 1939, it sparked quite the controversy. Large crowds gathered to stare at the strange composition, some interested, others disgusted and protesting that it was indecent. The manager of Bonwit Teller was nervous about the public reaction to the display window and decided to change it to something a little less sensual. When Salvador arrived at Bonwit Teller the following evening, he was appalled to discover that his mannequin and coals had gone and that his bathtub had been moved. In front of the gathering crowd, Salvador stormed furiously into the shop, whipped up into one of the temperamental rages that Felipa had to deal with when he was just a boy. Salvador seized his bathtub, bent on putting it back into place; unfortunately for Bonwit Teller, the artist was so fired up that he pushed the tub rather too hard. Instead of sliding back into place, it rocketed forward, slid out of Salvador's grasp, and smashed directly through the glass window and onto the street, much to the delight of the assembled crowd.

A notable exception to that was a police officer, who happened to be nearby. Salvador stumbled out of the hole in the window and straight into the cop's waiting grip. Luckily, his stay in prison was a short one. That same night, he was released, the magistrate pardoning Salvador on the grounds of his possessing an artistic temperament. This was undeniable, and Salvador was allowed to go free. The incident served only to increase Salvador's fame, as well as the spread of Surrealism in the United States.

While in New York, Salvador also took part in the New York World's Fair. He was given free license to design an exhibit, and this time, Salvador wasn't just going to hang up some paintings. Instead, he created his "Dream of Venus" pavilion.

"Dream of Venus" could not have been more out of place than at the World's Fair. The World's Fair was not an art exhibition at all; instead, the Fair had been designed to bring hope, rationality, and science to a world that was beginning to wonder not only what the future looked like, but also if there was going to be a future at all. 1939 was a bleak year to be alive, a time right on the very heels of the Great Depression. The Roaring Twenties had given way to darkness, fear, and the looming threat of a war that would claim millions of lives and change history forever. The World's Fair was about technological advancements, about bringing sense to a world that was about to lose its head with fear. A Surrealist exhibition was a questionable choice. Surrealism, however, was seen as the most modern form of art—and perhaps the organizers of the Fair realized that while science was necessary for humans to survive and understand, art was necessary for them to be human.

Levy, Salvador's constant American champion, was able to get his foot in the door with the Fair, and he designed one of his most extravagant works for this event. "Dream of Venus" was a pavilion, a so-called Surrealist funhouse with typical Dalí themes: heavily sexual, strangely hallucinatory, and deeply dreamlike. For the price of twenty-five cents, visitors could enter a chamber in the center of which a nude girl—representing Venus, the Roman goddess of love and a popular theme of Dalí art—lay stretched out on a red satin bed, apparently asleep and dreaming. Behind her, numerous paintings were hung, exhibiting many of Salvador's favorite themes and shapes: soft watches, burning giraffes, crutches, and pianos. The next part of the chamber was filled with all sorts of Surrealist objects, from cows to telephones to musical instruments to live models covered in fresh seafood.

"Dream of Venus" was significant, however, not only for its weirdness, especially when compared to the practical exhibits of the World's Fair, but also for the way it brought some of the most sophisticated art of the day to the average man on the street. In Salvador's time, art was for high society, not the common man. Surrealism, especially, with its hard-to-understand themes and strange shapes, was not something that ordinary people came into much contact with. However, the World's Fair allowed anyone with a quarter to walk right in and experience Surrealism at its finest. It brought art to the masses. And it made Salvador Dalí ridiculously famous.

After the World's Fair, Salvador and Gala both returned to Spain for the summer, despite the fact that the atmosphere in Europe had never been stormier. Hitler was secretly growing Germany's strength, training and arming troops despite the terms of the Versailles Treaty signed at the end of the First World War, as he was desperate to expand the territories of the German race so that it could grow and overrun the world as the only perfect race in existence. Hitler slowly sought alliances with similarly minded powers; Italy and the Soviet Union joined him, causing Great Britain and France to raise their hackles as they faced conflict with the mighty USSR. Mercifully, Franco, who had only just settled in as the dictator of Spain, chose to remain neutral instead of allying himself with Hitler.

Despite the tumultuous atmosphere, Salvador was able to continue painting happily in Port Lligat for a few more months. He continued to paint famous people such as Betty Stockfeld, Vermeer, Abraham Lincoln, and Freud. Another celebrity he painted in 1939 was Shirley Temple, the brilliant child star of *Rebecca of Sunnybrook Farm* (1938) and *The Little Princess* (1939). The title of his painting was *Shirley Temple: The Youngest, Most Sacred Monster of the Cinema in Her Time*, and it showed Temple's head on a red sphinx topped by a vampire bat.

Another famous person he painted was Hitler. This was the year that he would create *The Enigma of Hitler*, which contained a landscape in which he concealed Hitler's face. It appeared that the atrocities that the German ruler was committing were not enough to sway Salvador's obsession with him.

Whether or not Hitler knew that a Spanish Surrealist was painting him was probably not relevant to the German dictator at the time. He was much too busy making plans for war, and on September 1st, 1939, he put that war into action. Hitler gathered his troops and launched an invasion of Poland on that cold fall day, beginning the bitter, bloody six-year conflict that would dwarf even the Great War. France and Great Britain hurried to the defense of Poland, and the USSR soon joined Germany; the Second World War had begun.

Spain would remain neutral, although there was little in the way of neutrality in a war that encompassed so many countries and was fought upon so many continents. The beautiful seaside villa that Salvador loved so much and that had sheltered him and Gala even during the chaos of the Spanish Civil War was a safe haven no longer. They would have to flee. Salvador may have known this when he painted his last piece of 1939, *Telephone in a Dish With Three Grilled Sardines at the End of September.* The war had just begun, and this still life is strangely bleak and lifeless, quite unlike Salvador's normal vivid style. Perhaps this is how he felt facing the prospect of leaving his home behind, not knowing if he would ever see it again.

They left Port Lligat in early 1940, traveling first to Madrid and then to Cadaques one more time to visit Anna Maria and Salvador Senior. The world was a bleak place already, and when the bombs began to fall, Salvador knew they couldn't stay in Spain. He sent Gala ahead to secure her passage to safer lands and returned himself to Port Lligat. To his utter devastation, his beloved villa had been bombed.

Salvador needed someplace to go, somewhere to hide from the war and the falling bombs. France was out of the question, not with Salvador having just painted a masterpiece of Hitler. There was just one country that he knew would accept him with open arms despite his eccentricity, and that was the country that loved his eccentricity best: the United States of America. Getting there was easier said than done. Salvador had miles upon miles of war-torn territory to cross in order to make his way to safety. To complicate matters, thousands of people were trying to get out of Europe and flee to the US, particularly Jews who knew the Holocaust was upon them. However, Gala and Salvador managed to get to Bordeaux, where they were issued American visas and passage aboard the Portuguese ship *Excambion.* They set sail from Lisbon in the summer of 1940 and arrived in the safe haven of New York at last.

For Salvador, the first few months of 1940 had been terribly harsh. Port Lligat had been a place of decadence and luxury, filled with all the creature comforts to which Salvador was so addicted. During this period, he felt more like a homeless wanderer instead of the art world's greatest rock star. Arriving in New York, where WWII's slimy grip had not yet extended, Salvador Dalí returned to his flamboyant nature; he no longer had to be the man fleeing from war like a frightened animal. Reporters flocked to him, and Salvador settled back into his life as a rich and famous artist, safe from the death and destruction that was being sown in his homeland. Caresse Crosby, the bra inventor who'd supported Salvador since his first trip to New York City, was quick to offer him and Gala lodging at her Virginia home.

Salvador settled in at Caresse's beautiful house and began to paint. His first piece completed in the US was *Daddy Longlegs of the Evening... Hope!*, in which he expressed the desolation and despair he felt about the Second World War. A cannon spewing out a terrified, muscular horse and a molten biplane suggest violence and war; another of Dalí's soft self-portraits melts gently over a dead tree, playing a violin and supporting two inkwells, perhaps signifying the signing of a second treaty—one that, Salvador imagined, could have been as useless as the Treaty of Versailles. Ants crawl all over the head of the self-portrait. Perhaps Salvador felt that despair was eating his genius mind.

Arriving in the US, however, had rescued Salvador from total desolation. The entire painting is composed in dark and apocalyptic colors; even a despairing cupid, hunched in the corner of the scene, is composed in green and dark gray. But right at the center of the painting, in the middle of the self-portrait, is a splash of vibrant yellow, populated by a daddy longlegs. French custom had it that a daddy longlegs in the evening was not a symbol of war, chaos, death, or destruction but one of hope. While not as famous as *The Persistence of Memory* or *The Enigma of Desire*, this painting is one of Dalí's most emotionally charged and richly symbolic pieces.

Salvador went on to paint some more of his typical Surrealist compositions, including a portrait of Voltaire, the French Enlightenment poet, hidden among a slave market scene. But soon, the hope that Dalí felt as he composed *Daddy Longlegs* would fade back into black terror at the horrors unfolding in Europe. Norway, Denmark, Belgium, and the Netherlands had all been invaded by Germany; France was the next to fall, and the attack was disastrous. Britain was forced to evacuate from France, and Hitler took control over Paris on June 14th. Britain was heavily bombed, and it was only the Allied victory in the Battle of Britain that prevented Hitler from overrunning the island.

By the end of 1940, things looked utterly bleak for Europe. Salvador was obsessed with Hitler, but he wasn't German, and he knew what that would mean for him if he was to return to Europe with Hitler in control. Fear overwhelmed him, and that winter at Caresse's house, Salvador painted one of his most emotional pieces, *The Face of War*. Against a bare and lifeless desert, a corpse's face emits a silent scream of agony, its mouth and eye sockets filled with more corpses screaming, their mouths and eye sockets similarly filled into what appears to be infinity. It captures so much that those alive during World War II must have been feeling—the death, the emptiness, the agony, the terror, the feeling that it would never end, that it would never stop. Salvador, like millions of others, had been alive during the First World War. It must have felt almost apocalyptic to see it happen all over again, this time on an unprecedented scale of destruction.

In 1941, Salvador started to settle into life in the US a little more. He began to work on his autobiography, *The Secret Life of Salvador Dalí*, and on a novel. Finding work as a jewelry designer, Salvador discovered a new passion and threw himself into it. He created his jewelry masterpiece that year, known as the *Eye of Time*. This incredibly intricate brooch looks like a human eye, with a single bejeweled teardrop slipping out of it, until one looks closer and sees the hands of a watch on the iris.

He also worked with photographer Philippe Halsman and started to do some costume designing. Just as Picasso had designed the costumes for *Parade*, Salvador designed them for *Labyrinth*, which was also performed by the Ballets Russe. The Museum of Modern Art and Julien Levy's gallery continued to exhibit Salvador's paintings, and he continued to paint. These images were darker than before; they were less colorful than the vivid hues so evident in *The Persistence of Memory* and other earlier compositions, but they were, nonetheless, richly symbolic. He painted numerous portraits of Gala and a strangely realistic little oil painting called *The Original Sin*.

The word "sin," and the use of the biblical serpent in the painting, may point back to another profound shift that occurred in Salvador's psyche around the time that he returned to the US. He had always leaned more toward Salvador Senior's side when it came to religion, preferring atheism to his mother's devout Catholicism; Surrealism had tipped him further from religion, as it praised the human subconscious above any kind of order or morality. Yet something about the apocalyptic nature of the Second World War had forced Salvador to turn to something larger than himself for solace, the way he'd seen Felipa do countless times when he was a child. Although Salvador would never become a typical Catholic (he described himself as being "a Catholic without faith"), he started to turn back toward the Catholic Church during his time in the United States, and his strange approach to his renewed faith would be evident in many of his later masterpieces.

For eight years, Salvador and Gala mostly would remain in the United States, with only an occasional trip back to Europe—and they would only make these rare trips after the war. Salvador was a long way from his ancestral home, but he continued to work tirelessly on his art, becoming a major influence on the art fraternity in the United States and contributing to the fact that New York City became a center for arts and culture once the war was over. He published *The Secret Life of Salvador Dalí* in 1942; although it is known as his autobiography, it's uncertain how much of it is fact and how much is fiction. It certainly provided a fascinating glimpse into the psyche of a man who had become one of the 20th century's most famous and eccentric figures. He also wrote a novel in 1944, *Hidden Faces*, which was, of course, a Surrealist work featuring cars going to a fashion salon. Jewelry and costume design remained a major part of

Salvador's life, but, of course, painting was still his central passion. He made almost two hundred of his works during those years in the United States.

This was where religious figures first started to enter Salvador's art. One of the first was Saint George, as he slew his legendary dragon, in 1942; the Virgin Mary soon followed in numerous paintings, usually modeled, of course, by Gala. The war continued to influence many of the themes Salvador used as well. *Geopoliticus Child Watching the Birth of the New Man* (1943), which depicted a human figure struggling to emerge from a soft-shelled egg, was thought to symbolize the way in which the United States would affect global politics after the war.

By then, of course, the US had joined WWII on the Allied side after the Japanese attack on Pearl Harbor, and the war had erupted across Asia, Africa, Europe, and the Middle East. Hitler, having conquered most of Europe, had turned on the Soviet Union and attacked his erstwhile allies in 1941. The USSR had been placed under heavy pressure by the invading Germans, and with Great Britain and France occupied with heavy fighting in Europe, the United States was the only nation left that could engage Japan. American troops were sent to both the European and Pacific theaters of the war. It was now truly a global conflict. Salvador was inspired by America's contributions to the war, and he believed the great nation would become even greater in the wake of it if only victory could be secured.

Salvador painted some of his most important works in 1944, the year that the Allies launched their invasion of Europe and forced Hitler to send his men westward, which resulted in his defeat by the Soviets in Asia. Ancient Greek and Roman figures had also begun to appear in Salvador's work; *The Apotheosis of Homer* (1944) was one such painting. Another 1944 painting was perhaps Salvador's most recognizable after *The Persistence of Memory*. *Dream Caused by the Flight of a Bee Around a Pomegranate a Second Before Awakening* is an absolute masterpiece of technical skill and Surrealist composition. Against a background of Port Lligat—showing how deeply Salvador still yearned for his home by the sea—a serenely sleeping Gala levitates, unaware of the dangers crashing toward her. A pomegranate spews out a giant fish; the fish, in turn, coughs out two attacking tigers with bared teeth and rampant claws, and a rifle with a bayonet hovers just ahead of the tigers, the blade seemingly about to touch Gala's smooth skin. In the background, an elephant strolls across the sea on legs as long and thin as shadows. The piece is as beautiful and strange as it is frightening, with the vulnerability of Gala's nude figure so evident against the strong lines of her attackers. One can't help but wonder if Salvador feared everything that could harm Gala if the war went wrong—if the United States, their last refuge, fell. This painting, perhaps more than any of the other erotic and vibrant depictions of Gala, shows Salvador's genuine love and attachment for his wife.

Chapter 9 – Going Home

Illustration IV: Salvador and his pet ocelot

In 1945, Salvador Dalí painted *Basket of Bread*. The first time he had painted a still life of bread in a basket was in 1926 when he had just recently discovered Cubism and Surrealism and was still playing with different styles, looking for the medium that spoke to him most deeply. It had been nearly twenty years, and Salvador revisited the subject with technical brilliance and, strangely enough, no evidence of his usual Surrealist elements. The resultant painting is beautiful, almost muted, a still life that could have been composed by one of the classical masters instead of by the wild-eyed, pointy-mustached Salvador Dalí. It depicts the heel of a loaf of bread in a basket, poised on the edge of a table against a black backdrop. And while this painting may look like nothing but a skillful still life, to Salvador, it meant far, far more. The painting did not show Hitler's face, but its subtitle, *Rather Death Than Shame*, paid homage to the Nazi leader who was responsible for the war that claimed 75 million lives.

Salvador finished *Basket of Bread: Rather Death Than Shame* a single day before the end of the Second World War. The Allied invasion of France in 1944 had turned the tide of the terrible war; the Germans and Italians were beaten back again and again, and with terrible losses on both sides, the Allies finally pushed through to Berlin in early 1945. Adolf Hitler was unable to face the possibility of surrender. He committed suicide on April 30th, 1945, plummeting into the darkness that Salvador depicted as the backdrop in *Basket of Bread*.

The summer of 1945 was one of unprecedented violence. Germany surrendered, but Japan did not, and American blood flowed over Japanese earth in such profusion that the US decided it had no choice but to use the most destructive weapon in history—the atomic bomb. Hiroshima and Nagasaki were virtually destroyed by nuclear bombs in early August, and faced with the unimaginable loss of civilian life, Japan surrendered on September 2nd, 1945. It was the formal end of the devastating war.

While the fascist government of Hitler had been overthrown, fascism was not yet dead. Franco was still in command of Spain. It may be for this reason that Salvador did not hasten to return home once the war was over. He stayed in the US for three more years, composing several more masterpieces. Religious figures continued to populate his paintings; Catholicism had provided him with another wave of inspiration. Strangely enough, his next source of inspiration would be neither religion nor Surrealism. It would be science. The creation of the atomic bomb had ushered in a new era of nuclear physics, one that Salvador found utterly fascinating. For the rest of his career, he would explore a strange marriage between Catholic iconography and scientific elements, finding a path to what was known as nuclear mysticism—the explanation of the human consciousness with the science of nuclear physics. *Resurrection of the Flesh* (1945), *Madonna* (1946), and *The Temptation of St. Anthony* (1946) are all examples of paintings involving religious imagery. *The Temptation of St. Anthony* is one of Salvador's most famous works, using, once again, the symbol of elephants on long, stilted legs and rearing horses that terrify a naked, kneeling Saint Anthony, who holds up a cross to ward them off. It is a typical Dalí painting, dreamlike, vivid, and technically brilliant.

In 1946, he also painted the strangely peaceful and pretty composition *Noel*, depicting a picture-perfect Christmas scene complete with Christmas trees, snow, and baubles. Perhaps Salvador was starting to feel the world settle into peace after six years of horrific warfare. That year he made another film, this time collaborating with the greatest filmmaker of his time, Walt Disney. *Destino* was a six-minute short film that would only be released in 2003; it even won an Academy Award for Best Animated Short Film.

Salvador's stay in the United States had been hugely productive, but in 1948, he realized that it was time to return home. The war had been over for nearly three years, and Port Lligat was waiting. Salvador and Gala went home at last, despite the fact that the artist faced considerable backlash for going from the USA—home of the free—to fascist-controlled Spain.

Despite the fact that Spain itself had become the world's pariah, with the much-publicized war on fascism so terribly fresh in the collective consciousness, the years of Franco's dictatorship coincided with some of Salvador's happiest times. Franco himself was ridiculously repressive. He outlawed numerous religions and languages, including Catalan, had a secret police that carried out his oppressive regime, and ended up getting his entire country thrown out of the United Nations thanks to the secretive help he had given Hitler during the Second World War, despite Spain's ostensible neutrality. Spain's economy was poor, and its people were oppressed, but none of that could touch Salvador Dalí. Catholicism was the only religion that Franco failed to outlaw, and Salvador had more than enough money from his art that the failing economy had little effect on him. He was a supporter of Franco, and Salvador had actually met with the dictator and painted for him, so he was in no real danger. His haven in Port Lligat, which he expanded considerably during these years, felt like it was part of a different world. Salvador would say that time traveled more slowly in Port Lligat; the isolation and peace provided him with the perfect environment in which to create his art, and create he did.

Salvador became almost reclusive for the next twenty years, spending most of his time utterly immersed in his work. Gala held frequent and extravagant orgies and enjoyed the glamorous life of being Salvador Dalí's wife. Salvador himself, however, was busying himself with all kinds of art. The Second World War had left him a changed man. He was by no means devout, nor did he seem to pay particular attention to the commandments of his religion, but it certainly left an imprint on his art. Whether or not he really believed it, he was deeply fascinated with it. He continued to explore Catholicism and nuclear mysticism, going deeper than Freud's psychology and starting to explore larger themes than the human mind. Space, time, and immortality became his focus, with inspiration coming to him from science, religion, and mathematics.

In 1951, Salvador published his *Mystical Manifesto*, describing his theology of nuclear mysticism and how it affected his paintings and his beliefs. He felt that the invisible workings of the atom were inextricably linked to other invisible things, such as religion and human thinking, and it is this link that he explores in his later work.

His art was also changing in technicality. Salvador had long been a master, but in the 1950s and 1960s, he became a virtuoso. His technical skill was breathtaking, and he continued to build and expand upon it, studying the most advanced mathematics in order to bring those concepts to life in his art. He also started using new techniques and refining his use of old ones, such as foreshortening, negative space, visual puns, and optical illusions. He was also one of the first artists to use holography. Dennis Gabor had developed the holographic method—a way of projecting a three-dimensional image on a two-dimensional surface—in 1947, and the invention of the laser in 1960 catapulted the world into the age of the hologram. Salvador was the first person to see more than just science in the potential of the hologram. He met with Selwyn Lissack, a South African artist with a similar vision, in the 1970s, and they worked together to create several pieces of holographic art. The first and most well-known of these was *The Brain of Alice Cooper* (1973). Alice Cooper, a rock star, was considered by both himself and Salvador to be a Surrealist, and he was only too happy to be the subject of Salvador's first hologram. In 1969, Salvador also designed a logo for Chupa Chups, a Spanish lollipop brand whose logo remains an icon of the period.

The 1950s and 1960s were filled with all types of art, but, of course, painting remained Salvador's central focus. He spent most of his time buried in his work in Port Lligat, particularly producing his "Masterworks." These paintings are enormous, with the canvas stretching more than five feet in at least one direction, and they required a special slot in the floor of Salvador's custom-built studio in order for him to be able to work on them. One of the first of these was *The Madonna of Port Lligat*, which had been painted first in 1949 and then revisited again in 1950. This painting contains many of Salvador's key elements during his later period: Gala, as always, is his model, and there is also a basket of bread, an ostrich egg, and a rhinoceros. The rhinoceros, thanks to its horn growing in a logarithmic spiral, would become an increasingly popular motif in his work.

Leda Atomica (1949) is another prelude to Salvador's nuclear mysticism period. The image was inspired by the Greek mythology of Leda, the queen of Sparta, who was seduced by the Greek god Zeus. However, there's more to the painting than just a vividly lifelike portrait of Leda (inspired, of course, by Gala) with a swan and several other components floating in midair, apparently disconnected. It was created based on the mathematical framework of a six-pointed star set inside a pentagon, which Salvador called the "divine proportion." The great master of the surreal had turned to logic, and yet even logic melted in his fingers, with the highest planes of science becoming dreamlike and mystical when he pinned them to his canvas.

In 1951, Salvador painted *A Logician Devil* as part of his illustrations for Dante's *Divine Comedy*. The following year, he revisited his great masterpiece, *The Persistence of Memory*, in *The Disintegration of the Persistence of Memory*, which explores the new scientific theme of matter breaking down into its individual atoms by splitting the masterpiece up into brick-like blocks. He also painted *Galatea of the Spheres* that year, a portrait of Gala composed of spheres that never touch, exploring how all matter is composed of roughly spherical atoms. *The Sacrament of the Last Supper* (1955) shows Christian icons, not dissimilar to those in Leonardo da Vinci's *The Last Supper*, slowly fading into transparency. It is the most popular painting in Washington DC's National Gallery of Art to this day.

The Discovery of America by Christopher Columbus (1959) may not be the most well-known of Salvador's Masterworks, but it is certainly one of the biggest, standing at fourteen feet high. It intricately depicts the moment that Columbus arrived in what he believed was India but actually turned out to be a Caribbean island. Beautiful, harmonious, and lacking the sense of the grotesque that is so prevalent in some of Salvador's other paintings, this piece hearkens back to one of Salvador's earliest influences—Diego Velázquez, the portrait master himself.

In 1953, Francis Crick and James D. Watson made tremendous progress in the science of genetics by discovering the double helix of DNA. Salvador was wildly inspired, not only by the concept of DNA but also by its incredible shape. He honored Crick and Watson with his painting *Galacidalacidesoxiribunucleicacid* (1963), whose amazing title is a combination of Gala's name, the word "Allah" (Arabic for "God"), and deoxyribonucleic acid (DNA). The painting itself is created in soft shades, exploring linked themes between the resurrection of Christ and the discovery of DNA.

The Hallucinogenic Toreador (1968-70) is a more typical Dalí painting, with brilliant colors, grotesque shapes, and a nightmarish quality. It was inspired by Gala's hatred of the violent sport of bullfighting, and it is one of Salvador's last great masterpieces.

The Masterworks were not the only art that Salvador was working on during this period, however. He was immersed in designing both costumes and décor for various ballets, and he also turned his hand to writing, publishing articles in both French and English magazines such as *Connaissance des Arts* and *Vogue*. In 1962, he published another book, *The World of Salvador Dalí*. This was published and widely read in the United States, and so, Salvador traveled to Manhattan in order to attend a book signing. Of course, because he was Salvador, he didn't simply sign his books like a normal person. When buyers arrived at the store to meet with the legendary Dalí, they were not disappointed, as his blood pressure and brainwaves were being measured by a machine, which produced printouts of the data it gathered. Each buyer was presented with a printout alongside their signed copy.

Even though Salvador was spending most of his time happily creating in Port Lligat, he was still actively engaging in his usual publicity stunts, like driving around with a car full of cauliflower, drinking from an ant-infested swan's egg, or happily urinating on a painting recently gifted to him by rising star Andy Warhol in the bar of the St. Regis Hotel, where Salvador had been staying since his first visit to New York. He'd also become a well-known figure on television screens all over the world. In 1960, he produced his documentary, *Chaos and Creation*, bringing his methods—including the paranoiac-critical method—to the world. He also starred in numerous television commercials and other marketing campaigns. One, an advertisement for French chocolate, had him saying, "I'm crazy about Lanvin chocolate!" while pulling a funny face. The public loved it; Salvador had long been known as being a mad genius, and that was just fine with him.

"If you've got it, flaunt it!" has become a well-used phrase in the modern day, and it is wonderfully fitting that the ever-arrogant Salvador was an important part of the marketing campaign that made the phrase famous. Despite the fact that many artists—Surrealists, in particular—were derisive of Salvador's flamboyant habits and commercial motives, their protests fell on deaf ears. Even when André Breton started calling Salvador Dalí "Avida Dollars" (meaning "eager for dollars"), Salvador largely ignored him. He was rolling in money, living in the lap of luxury, and an international celebrity. He didn't need André Breton's approval, and Breton died in 1966 without giving it to him. The Surrealist movement, more or less, died with him, as the organization was long gone by then. Surrealism itself lived on, just as Salvador had said, in the art of Salvador Dalí.

Surrealist art would continue to be brought to the public even though its founder had passed away; Salvador would make sure of it. From 1961 to 1974, Salvador's main focus was his Dalí Theatre-Museum in Figueres, his old hometown. The museum is still a popular tourist attraction to this day, and even the architecture is profoundly Surrealist, with a domed roof topped by giant eggs.

In 1964, Salvador was awarded the Cross of the Order of Isabella the Catholic, the highest honor Spain could bestow upon him. His work, by this point, had been exhibited all over the world, including Europe, America, and even as far away as Japan.

Now that Salvador was more or less Catholic, he also felt that something was missing in his marriage to Gala. They had been civilly married since 1934, but by 1958—24 years into their marriage—

Salvador was troubled by the fact that they were not married in the eyes of the Catholic Church. Despite his sacrilegious art and his utter disregard of many Christian customs, Salvador felt strongly about the holiness of love. "It's the sacredness that's important," he said. "I want the world to know how sacred love is."

He and Gala were married a second time in 1958, with Gala having obtained a special dispensation from the pope due to her status as a divorcee. She herself was a devout Catholic, and so, they had all the pomp of a splendid Catholic wedding, which Salvador found to fit his taste perfectly. It was almost thirty years since he had met Gala; he had been an agonized, aimless 25-year-old then. Now he was 55, wandering off the precipice of middle age, but he was still vividly and furiously in love with her. She'd been his muse for so long that he hardly knew what life would be without her.

Thirteen years after their church wedding, Salvador would be forced to find out.

Chapter 10 – Farewell to the Muse

Salvador would have given Gala anything she wanted. What she wanted, it turned out, was a castle.

Of course, Salvador wouldn't deny her the request, and he had more than enough money to make it happen. He started to search the length and breadth of Spain for a castle fit for a muse and discovered it at last in the village of Pubol, a little less than forty miles from Port Lligat. The small castle, built in the 12th century, was badly neglected and rundown, but there was something inexpressibly romantic about its round towers and ancient walls, something fairytale-like that inspired Salvador and made him feel that it was the perfect home for Gala. He bought Pubol Castle in 1968 and got to work renovating it and turning it into a Surrealist palace for his beloved Gala. It was not as flamboyant and colorful as the house at Port Lligat, as it had more of Gala's personal taste than Salvador's, but it did contain many artworks that Salvador created solely for his beloved wife. It was complete with a mausoleum and a throne room, in which there stood a single throne—Gala's.

Today, the Gala-Dalí Castle is open to the public as a museum of Salvador's art and life. In 1971, when Gala moved to the castle, it was shut tight, even to her own husband. Things had soured between Salvador and Gala since their wedding in 1958; Salvador, it would appear, remained hopelessly in love with Gala, but her heart had turned cold against him just as it did with Éluard, Ernst, and her own daughter Cecile. While Gala spent some of her time at Port Lligat with Salvador, she would retreat to her castle for months in the summer. Salvador was not allowed to accompany her. In fact, he was not even allowed to visit her except by her prior written invitation.

Perhaps worst for Salvador was the fact that Gala was not alone in Pubol. Instead, she entertained herself with strings of young lovers. As careful as she had always been with her money, Gala was now lavish and extravagant, spending Salvador's cash on the men with whom she committed adultery against him. Gala was now in her late sixties; her time as a young and glamorous icon of the Surrealist movement was gone just like the movement itself, but she refused to let go of everything that her youth and beauty had given her. She was now the famous and fabulously eccentric wife of an equally eccentric painter. Gala Dalí had never been denied what she wanted. She wasn't about to start now.

Salvador, in turn, continued to hold orgies at Port Lligat and invite beautiful young women to visit him, but his heart wasn't in it. He had always feared physical contact, even with Gala; his love was for her beauty, and according to some accounts, his desire for her would always be unrequited despite decades of marriage. He could not bring himself to lay his hands on the girls who came to Port Lligat. Even if he could, it wasn't their bodies he wanted—it was their beauty. But none of them could inspire him the way that Gala did. Nothing, not science, not art, not psychology, would ever be the same kind of muse to him as a single beloved woman.

Gala had all but left him, but it didn't stop Salvador from painting her. She was still his muse, even if she no longer loved him. In 1972, he painted *Dalí from the Back Painting Gala from the Back Eternalized by Six Virtual Corneas Provisionally Reflected in Six Real Mirrors*. The painting was never quite finished, but its muted colors still speak of something faded, something a little lost. It is extraordinarily lifelike, but it is not lively; there is something real, grounded, and tragic about it that is missing in Salvador's earlier work.

The dreamlike quality is gone. Everything about this painting is heartbreakingly real, such as Salvador's thinning hair and Gala's cold expression, and immortalized in exquisite technique. It may not contain the terror of *The Face of War* or the complicated symbols of *The Madonna of Port Lligat*, but this obscure painting is one of Salvador's most emotionally charged.

He continued to paint Surrealist images as well: *Gala's Dream* (1972), *Hitler Masturbating* (1973), and *Wounded Soft Watch* (1974) are just a few examples. 1974 was also the year that the Dalí Theatre-Museum was opened for the first time, and it remains open to this day, owning one of the largest collections of Salvador's work. Another important collection, the Salvador Dalí Museum, was opened in 1971 in Ohio.

In the 1970s, Salvador also experimented with yet another medium of making art: the photomosaic. Now a popular method of creating art, photomosaics are made by using "tiles" made up of small images to create a larger image. *Gala Contemplating the Mediterranean Sea which at a distance of 20 meters is transformed into the portrait of Abraham Lincoln (Homage to Rothko)* (1974) and *Lincoln in Dalívision* (1977) are both examples of Salvador's photomosaics. Although his health was failing—being separated from Gala had catapulted Salvador into a state of depression that was deeply detrimental to his health—Salvador never stopped experimenting with new methods. He plunged deeper and deeper into the realm of mathematics, seeking theories and equations to further deepen his artwork. In the 1970s, he also started producing stereoscopic paintings, including Dalí lifting the skin of the Mediterranean to show gala the birth of Venus (1977) and the chair (1976). He also experimented with random dot painting, producing randomdot correlogram – the golden fleece in 1977. Spheres, surrealism, and famous people continued to be themes in his work; he painted Marilyn Monroe in 1972, inventor dr. Brian mercer in 1973, and an equestrian portrait of Francisco Franco's daughter in 1974. He also illustrated one of Sigmund Freud's books, despite the fact that he had moved beyond the foundation that Freud's writings had given him and into a whole new world of art and thinking.

Salvador's work would only stop when his hands grew too weak to hold a brush, and by the late 1970s, those days were coming nearer, and all of his greatest masterpieces were behind him. He was losing his hair; his iconic mustache had turned gray, and his health was growing worse and worse as all his old fears of abandonment and loss came back to haunt him now that gala was gone for long stretches of time. To make matters worse, gala herself was no longer young. By 1980, Salvador was 76; gala was an octogenarian, and although Salvador still saw her as the most beautiful woman in the world, she was no longer as mentally present as she had been before. Dementia was beginning to afflict gala, and while this meant that Salvador saw her more often since she could no longer be left alone for long periods, it must have been heart-wrenching for him to see her sharp intellect begin to fade.

Or maybe it wasn't. According to some accounts, as Salvador grew older and sicker, his longing for gala and fear of losing her turned to rage. By this point, gala had had an affair with rock star Jeff Fenholt, who was about fifty years her junior. Her ability to manage money—always extravagant Salvador's saving grace—had faded. Now she spent money freely on whatever she wanted or whatever her lovers wanted, while Salvador pined for her. During one of the rare times when the couple was actually together, Salvador finally snapped. He was old, sick, and running out of money thanks to being conned out of the profits of much of his work, and the person he loved deeply had betrayed him. The sadistic streak that had been so evident when Salvador was a boy came right back to him, and he fell upon gala, who had for so long been the object of his greatest affections, with utterly shocking violence. She was old and frail, and his furious beating broke two of her ribs.

Gala was old and senile, but even in her twilight years, even after being viciously beaten by her husband, she was no victim. Once she returned home after recovering from her injuries, she briskly set about taming the savage beast that had apparently taken over her once-loving husband. Her solution was to dose him with large amounts of prescription medication. Unfortunately, in her senility, gala didn't sedate her husband. She poisoned him.

Tragically, the greatest damage was to Salvador's nervous system. He began to experience tremors in his right hand, which was his painting hand. The larger-than-life persona who had pushed a bathtub through a New York boutique window, graced the cover of time, and brought surrealism across the Atlantic ocean was reduced to a frail, balding old man whose right hand shook every time he tried to paint.

Nonetheless, Salvador continued to work, shaky hand and all. In 1980, he only made six paintings, but through the rest of the early eighties, he continued to work as well as he could, although his days of producing masterpieces were long gone. In fact, Salvador never retired; he would paint until his deathbed.

Not even the loss of his muse would stop him. Even though gala didn't leave Salvador after her beating or during his illness, she was very old and growing gradually sicker, and Salvador knew that he was losing her. Even as he contemplated his own immortality (a belief that grew as he aged), he was watching his muse fade away before his eyes. That bright-eyed, smiling, vivacious woman who had elbowed her way into the surrealist movement and captured his heart was now on her last legs. It didn't stop her from continuing her affair with Fenholt, but despite his rage, neither did it stop Salvador from caring for her. She was at home in port Iligat with him when she contracted a case of influenza. A disease so easily shaken off by the young and healthy, the flu proved to be too much for the aging gala. She died on June 10th, 1982, beside the summery blue waters of the home she had once loved. She and Salvador had been together for more than half a century. He buried her in the mausoleum he had built for her underneath the castle she had loved.

The loss of gala was an awful blow for Salvador, one that seemed to catapult him from dazzling brilliance into doddering old age. His will to live was leached out of him. Gala had been his lifeblood, the electricity in his veins, his desire to paint, his greatest obsession. He had not treated her well at times, but she had still been everything to him. Salvador began to refuse food or water; he engaged in self-harm, scratching at his face as if the pain and bleeding could somehow make gala come back. Dehydration sucked at him, threatening to kill him, and his caregivers struggled to persuade him to care for himself. Even though his mind was beginning to fade, Salvador's fierce intelligence still sought for a solution to his agony. While his refusal of food or water may have been a suicide attempt, some say that Salvador was attempting to put himself into a state of suspended animation, like a toad in ice. He was just trying to escape. To rest. To get away from a world without gala Dalí.

Chapter 11 – The Marquis' Last Drawing

Illustration V: The Dalí Theatre-Museum, where Salvador Dalí's body is buried.

General Francisco Franco breathed his last on November 20th, 1975. Heart failure claimed "El Caudillo"–"the leader"–and left his country open to tentatively nose its way toward freedom. Franco's fascism had faded as the years went on, and the more modern times and ideas wore away at his oppressive tendencies; by the time he stepped down and nominated his successor, Spain was working toward becoming a democracy, and its first elections were held only two years after his death.

Spain had grown free and peaceful. Its most famous artist, however, was anything but.

Even the beloved views, still waters, and smooth beaches of Port Lligat could no longer soothe Salvador's heart. The landscapes of Cadaques had inspired and calmed him ever since he was a little boy playing with the Pichot children and learning about what modern art was, in a world before the First World War, before the atomic bomb, before Salvador Dalí. But now, with Gala gone, life had lost its savor. Salvador didn't want to gaze at the gorgeous views or paint the rocky crags again. He just wanted to be with Gala, and the only way he could think of to do that was to return to Pubol Castle where his wife was buried. He had built two graves in the mausoleum, only a small distance apart, saying that he wished to hold hands with Gala in death. Perhaps he would gladly have done so, but he couldn't. He was cursed with the affliction of living when everything he lived for was gone, and so, he went on, and for as long as he lived, he also painted.

Here, in his last paintings, it is most evident that art wasn't something Salvador Dalí did; it was something he *was*. He could no more give up painting than he could give up breathing. He found inspiration in Michelangelo's work, creating Surrealist versions of some of the old master's greatest paintings, and he also painted a fascinating, contorted, twisted version of El Escorial, one of Madrid's most important pieces of architecture.

When Gala died, though he had abused her, he was still painting her. Salvador painted a piece called *The Three Glorious Enigmas of Gala*. This time, though, the great master couldn't finish. Even though he could have drawn her from his heart's memory, he couldn't bring himself to finish painting Gala one last time. He couldn't be done with her.

Exploded Head is another 1982 painting, perhaps a vision of how shattered Salvador's mind felt from the grief of losing Gala. *Hysterical*

Venus de Milo was sculpted in 1982 and 1983, showing Venus melting mid-scream, a contorted testimony to the wild depths of sorrow. He also painted *Martyr*, showing how he felt, that he'd been crucified on the cross of his own life, his hands refusing to make art the way they used to, his muse gone, his life meaningless. His art had lost its piercingly realistic quality; his hands could no longer master those perfect brushstrokes. Now he mostly sketched, in raw and runny colors, with sweeping curves still showing the skill of the maestro as he tried to bring his dreams to life. They were just sketches, though. They weren't dream-photographs the way they once had been.

The Swallow's Tail, painted in 1983, was Salvador Dalí's last painting. Unlike many of his other late paintings, this one maintained sharp, clean lines and the incredible technique that had made Salvador's paintings less abstract than they were pure magic. A fairly simple composition, *The Swallow's Tail* is nonetheless loaded with symbolism. It was based on mathematician René Thom's mathematical catastrophe theory, a complex theory involving the fourth dimension. Salvador called it "the most beautiful aesthetic theory in the world," and of course, shaky hands or not, he just had to paint it. He brought the theory to life in *The Swallow's Tail*, mingling mathematical equations and geometric lines with the soft folds of a napkin and the smooth curves of a cello.

After *The Swallow's Tail*, Salvador would never pick up his oil paints again. He did produce some lithographs, however, but just how many—and which ones—is unclear. Some accounts say that Salvador purposely signed blank sheets of lithograph paper, allowing vast amounts of forgeries to be created in his name.

Salvador continued to sketch and doodle, particularly warriors on horseback often fighting with musical instruments. Stumbling around his castle home, he painted, missed Gala, and waited to die. One bright spark in his twilight years was the Spanish royal family. King Juan Carlos I, the man who had paved Spain's way to democracy and defended that democracy when it was still in its fragile early years, had long been a fan of Salvador's art. In 1982, the king decided that it was high time that Salvador was honored with a rank of nobility. King Juan Carlos gave Salvador the title of Marquis of Pubol Castle. Although the king originally wanted this title to be hereditary, there would have been little point, as Salvador never had any children. Perhaps showing the last flash of his old narcissism, Salvador requested that the title should be his and his alone, never to pass on to anyone else. The king honored this request in 1983, and Salvador was thus the first and last Marquis of Pubol.

Another bright part of Salvador's life was his friendship with a younger French filmmaker, Robert Descharnes. Twenty-two years Salvador's junior, Robert had collaborated with him on numerous works, and he had become a loyal supporter and kind companion as Salvador slipped into old age. His book, *Dalí*, is widely considered one of the best references for Salvador's real life and personality—it is definitely far more trustworthy than Salvador's own autobiography, which was largely fabricated. Robert was a frequent visitor at Pubol Castle, especially since Salvador had appointed him in 1980 to help with running his art firm and preventing forgeries from overflowing the market. As Salvador would discover in 1984, this was a good thing. Robert was a friend who was about to become a hero.

Salvador was no longer dehydrating himself and appeared to have resigned himself to living out the rest of his days peacefully at Pubol—at least, that is how it seemed. The old Surrealist, however, may have had other ideas.

It was four o'clock on the morning of August 30th, 1984, when Pubol Castle caught fire. Salvador, despite being a weak and emaciated octogenarian requiring round-the-clock care, was unattended in his room when the flames caught on the thick hangings of his four-poster bed. The flames ravaged them, reducing them to hot ash that tumbled onto the ancient artist where he lay, searing through his skin, burning him. Salvador was on fire, just like the giraffes in his paintings, and he was too old and helpless to escape. He began to scream, and Robert Descharnes was the one who heard. Rushing into the smoke, Robert managed to drag Salvador from his burning bed and take him to Gala's Cadillac. While it's unclear exactly what happened next, it's likely that Robert wanted to take Salvador to Barcelona for immediate hospital treatment. Salvador's legs and arms were covered in hideous burns, some of them right through the skin.

But Salvador was insistent. He wanted to go to Figueres. He wanted to go to his museum and see the progress of an exhibit there. One cannot imagine why Robert relented—perhaps the old painter was as stubborn as he was eccentric, or perhaps Robert thought he was dying and wanted to grant his last request—but either way, the badly burned Salvador was soon on his way to his beloved museum. He was carried into the museum on a stretcher, where he gazed at everything, muttering quietly, "We must do more things. We must do more things!" His art was all that he had left to hold on to.

Finally, Robert was able to take him to the hospital in Barcelona. The doctors were horrified to see his condition. Salvador was not only badly burned but emaciated and malnourished; allegations of neglect were bandied around, although it's unclear whether Salvador was being neglected by his nurses or by himself. He underwent emergency treatment, including a skin graft on 20% of his body, showing how severe the burns really were. The fact that he had made it to the hospital was incredible, and the media went mad all over the world about the news. It was thought that Salvador was on his deathbed, and the whole world waited for the eighty-year-old painter to die.

But he didn't die. Salvador survived, and his friends moved him away from Pubol and into his beloved museum in Figueres, ensuring that he was given better care and provided with everything he wanted in his last days. In fact, Salvador even continued to draw after the fire. In 1984, he had helped to illustrate a new edition of *Alice in Wonderland*; he also designed numerous sculptures, from the graceful *The Dance of Time* to the *Profile of Time*, the latter which shows a soft watch draped over a dead tree. After the fire, he was no longer working seriously, but he still doodled whenever he could and produced numerous sketches and even designs for playing cards.

1985 was Salvador's last productive year as an artist. He grew older and sicker, requiring a pacemaker to be implanted as his heart began to fail, and yet the suicide attempts had ceased. Instead, Salvador seemed to claw back some of his old egocentricity. His near-death experience had not made him aware of his own mortality; instead, since he had survived, he began to believe himself immortal. The great Dalí, he reasoned, could never die.

He was in and out of the hospital at the end of 1988, but he still managed to make his last visit to his museum in January 1989. It is difficult to interpret the statement Salvador made to the waiting media there. They could have been the words of a man who believed he was immortal, or they could have been those of a man who was tired of life. Either way, they were very much Salvador Dalí in their dramatic nature.

"When you are a genius, you do not have the right to die," he said, "because we are necessary for the progress of humanity."

It is undeniable that Salvador contributed, in his own unique and sometimes questionable way, to the progress of humanity. And the right to die was not denied him. He was 84 years old, and his life was ticking away, melting like one of his clocks. When he returned to the hospital after his visit, it was clear that Salvador was never coming out again.

One of his last visitors was King Juan Carlos himself, who came to see him in December 1988, shortly before Salvador went back to the museum for the last time. Salvador was grateful to see the king, and his mind was still fairly lucid. He offered to draw something for Juan Carlos and was provided with a pen and paper, on which his shaking old hands drew the last piece of art that he would ever create, bringing a final piece of his creativity into the world. *Head of Europa* was his last drawing.

Although his life had been extravagant and busy and loud, Salvador's death was quiet and peaceful. His caregivers had put on his favorite record for him, *Tristan and Isolde*. The old piece of Arthurian legend played in his hospital room, perhaps evoking memories of a happier time, a time when he had provided décor for the play of that name in the early 1940s. And so, without fuss, the old artist slipped peacefully from this life on January 23rd, 1989.

Somewhat tragically, Salvador Dalí was not buried next to Gala the way he had wished. Instead, he is buried in the crypt of the Dalí Theatre-Museum, less than a quarter-mile from the house where he was born and across the street from the church where he was given his first communion as a little boy under Felipa's adoring eyes.

Chapter 12 – The Immortal Mustache

When they dug up Salvador Dalí, they weren't expecting to see his mustache.

Dalí had been dead for 28 years. There couldn't be anything left of him, officials thought, as they lifted the one-and-a-half-ton slab from the top of his crypt and began the slow and painstaking process of exhuming an art hero's body. Already the very act was a violation of Dalí's dignity and privacy, as protested by many of his admirers and the Gala-Salvador Dalí Foundation. But one can imagine that, if Dalí had been able to see what happened next, he would have loved it because the thing that embalmer Narcís Bardalet took out of the crypt was not just a corpse. It was the body of Salvador Dalí, and a little bit of his magic seemed to have clung to it, to have outlived the artist himself. When Bardalet lifted an ornate napkin from Dalí's frozen face, there it was, looking back up at him, pointing upward as ever and perfectly curled: the Dalí mustache, which had become a symbol for art everywhere.

It was a little gray, for sure, and a little dusty, but the mustache was perfectly preserved. Airtight conditions in the crypt had prevented it from decaying, and the keratin in Dalí's famed facial hair was able to withstand almost thirty years underground.

The news caused an instant media sensation, the type that Dalí had always loved. The whole world loved the idea that the mustache was still intact, and even though he'd been dead for decades, Salvador Dalí was making headlines one last time.

It had all started with María Pilar Abel Martínez. A tarot card reader and TV psychic from Spain, Abel was also a serial plaintiff. Her first lawsuit was against Spanish writer Javier Cercas, whose novel *Soldiers of Salamis* deals with the effect on his country's psyche of the Spanish Civil War. His book is critically acclaimed and widely read, but it also depicts a fortune-teller named Conchi. Abel claimed to feel insulted by the way Cercas handled the character and took him to court for it, demanding 600,000 euros (about 660,000 US dollars) in reparations. Cercas didn't know Abel from a bar of soap, and the judge dismissed the case.

This didn't deter Abel from trying once again to file a lawsuit against a high-profile defendant. Two years after the Cercas case, Abel laid a claim in a Madrid court that she had the right to one-quarter of Salvador Dalí's estate, which was being handled by the Gala-Salvador Dalí Foundation and reputed to have been worth several hundred million euros. Why would an ordinary tarot card reader have a claim to this lucrative estate? Because, Abel claimed, she was Salvador Dalí's daughter.

Her claim made headlines all over the world as those who had known Dalí protested that it was utterly impossible for him to have fathered a child. He had always claimed to be impotent, for one thing; there was also the fact that he feared physical contact and may never even have been intimate with his own wife. Yet Abel's case was convincing enough that the court had no choice but to investigate it. Abel's mother, Antonia, had been working for a family who lived near the Dalí retreat in Cadaques in the 1950s. What was more, Abel bore a striking physical resemblance to Salvador. "All that's missing is a mustache," she is quoted as saying. Abel's mother had told her when she was a child that Salvador Dalí was her father and that Antonia had had an affair with him while he was married to Gala. Abel's grandmother affirmed this story, saying, "You are the daughter of a great painter, but I love you all the same." She went on to tell Abel that she is "odd," just like her reported father.

The case was bandied back and forth for a full ten years as Abel's lawyer fought for a piece of Dalí's enormous estate. In early 2017, the judge ruled that the only way to solve the case would be to obtain samples of Dalí's tissue to test his DNA against Abel's. To the utter horror of the Gala-Salvador Dalí Foundation, the only way to get these samples would be to dig up Salvador Dalí's body.

The exhumation, with its surprising discovery of Dalí's intact mustache, was hotly contested by local authorities and by the foundation. Authorities stated that proper procedure had not been followed, but Abel and her lawyer were insistent—the tests would be done, and Dalí would be exhumed. Samples were taken of his hair and bone, and the paternity tests were run while Dalí's body was kept outside of the crypt.

In September 2017, the test results came back. They were final and conclusive: there was absolutely no relation between Salvador Dalí and María Pilar Abel Martínez. Abel's case was dismissed by the court, and she was ordered to pay the legal fees incurred, which, considering that the exhumation was a lengthy process, amounted to around seven thousand euros.

Abel went away empty-handed and enraged from another failed lawsuit. As for Dalí, the samples taken from his body were carefully returned to him, and his body was laid to rest once more beneath the stage of the museum he loved.

The Gala-Salvador Dalí Foundation maintained control over Dalí's estate. Dalí had started the foundation in 1983, knowing that his time was short and that he would not have any children to inherit his considerable fortune, and the foundation had been rescued by Robert Descharnes after all of Salvador's and Gala's squandering. The foundation is responsible for running four museums: the Dalí Theatre-Museum, where Salvador's body is buried; the Dalí-Jewels, where his jewelry collection is on display; and two home museums at Dalí's residences, Port Lligat and Pubol.

These Dalí museums have become important tourist attractions in Catalonia, and they're not the only ones. The Museum of Modern Art in New York City still contains *The Persistence of Memory*, which is arguably its most popular piece. Founded in 1971, the Salvador Dalí Museum that originally stood in Ohio has now found its permanent home in St. Petersburg, Florida.

Salvador Dalí's legacy lives on, and not just in his miraculously preserved mustache. Though the Surrealists excommunicated him, Dalí is still arguably the most famous Surrealist who ever lived, and his influence helped the ideas of Surrealism to endure far beyond the death of André Breton—and even of Dalí himself. Today, many painters cite him as their greatest inspiration, among them Jeff Koons, who sculpts balloon animal shapes out of shining metal; singer and artist Yoko Ono, John Lennon's widow and a respected artist in her own right; and the late Andy Warhol, the creator of some of the modern world's most recognizable images.

Salvador Dalí did more than just inspire artists to make art. He also inspired artists to become more than just faceless signatures in the corner of a canvas but a brand in and of themselves. His flamboyant persona was almost as much of a selling point as the paintings themselves. Ultimately, Salvador Dalí showed the world that his paintings, objects, films, sculptures, and writings were only a tiny part of his artistry. The real masterpiece was himself.

Conclusion

Salvador Dalí stood for many things, and Surrealism was only one of them. He was a mad scientist who worked in a studio instead of a laboratory; a temperamental artist, whose medium ranged from the human psyche to nuclear physics; a crowd-loving clown, whose audience was the artistic fraternity and who worked on headlines instead of inside a big top.

Ultimately, while Dalí had an incredible effect on art, his greatest effect was on people. He influenced art for the rest of history, and he influenced people as well, filling up memories in his time and remaining an icon in ours. And the joyous thing about Dalí is that he did all of this without having to make sense. He introduced a splash of color into a world torn apart by war, bringing a little of the absurd into a world that was making leaps and bounds in science. While scientists were splitting the atom and putting men on the moon, Dalí was painting melting clocks and women filled with drawers.

The 20th century was, in many ways, defined by its suffering. With two World Wars, the Cold War, and the Great Depression to deal with, it was a harsh time. Logic and reason were, for many, the only things that they could trust. When the world was crumbling, humanity clung to what it could understand.

Except for that piece of humanity known as Salvador Dalí. Dalí sought for absurdity, for things that didn't need to be explained, and he found joy and hope in it. He turned boiled beans into a premonition of war and telephones into a sex symbol, and none of it needed to make sense. Salvador reveled in his own complete lack of reason and celebrated madness and the ridiculous. And as much as the world needed the cold, hard-edged minds that would make sense out of the senseless—as much as the world needed Freud and Churchill—it also needed a mind that could melt. A mind that could warp reality and distort the way humanity perceives space, time, and logic. A mind that was not obsessed with making sense out of the senseless but with making the senseless beautiful.

That mind belonged to Salvador Dalí. Controversial though he was, strange though he was, enigmatic though he remains, he brought something indefinable to his era that was desperately needed. He was not necessarily the greatest thinker of his time, but he was definitely one of the greatest dreamers. And like all great dreamers, though he might not have changed history, he changed humanity forever.

Here's another book by Captivating History that you might be interested in

Links to More Pictures of Famous Spanish Paintings (By Dalí and Others)

https://www.nationalgallery.org.uk/artists/francisco-de-zurbaran
http://www.artnet.com/artists/francisco-de-zurbar%C3%A1n/
http://www.diego-Velázquez.org/
http://www.franciscogoya.com/index.jsp
https://www.timeout.com/newyork/art/best-picasso-paintings-and-sculptures-ranked
https://www.Dalípaintings.com/
http://www.all-art.org/art_20th_century/Dalí-5.html
https://www.salvador-Dalí.org/en/Dalí-foundation/ - The Gala-Salvador Dalí Foundation

Glossary

Abstract - A style of art that depicts real objects in an unconventional manner by suggesting at their form with unrealistic colors or shapes.

Avant-garde - Used to describe art or ideas that are new and often unconventional or experimental.

Expressionism - A style of art that seeks to express emotion instead of outward reality.

Foreshortening - A technique used in art whereby the artist creates the illusion of an object extending into the distance.

Impressionism - An art style that aims to capture a powerful visual impression of a real subject rather than a fully realistic depiction of that subject.

Landscape - An artwork depicting a setting, usually of nature.

Perspective - In art, the technique of depicting three-dimensional objects on a two-dimensional canvas or other surface.

Portrait - An artwork depicting a person.

Random dot painting - Paintings that use an apparently random series of dots to inspire an abstract depiction of a subject.

Realism - The style of art in which a subject is portrayed to look as near as possible to the real thing.

Still life - An artwork depicting an arrangement of inanimate objects.

Surrealism - An art movement that encouraged the use of the subconscious to create dreamlike, almost hallucinatory works of art. Many of these were hyper-realistic depictions of highly unrealistic subjects.

Stereoscopic - A technique in which two images of the same object, made at different angles, are brought together to create an illusion of depth.

Sources

Henley, L. 2018, *Who were the Neanderthals?*, Natural History Museum, viewed 30 January 2020, <https://www.nhm.ac.uk/discover/who-were-the-neanderthals.html>

Greshko, M. 2018, *World's Oldest Cave Art Found – and Neanderthals Made It,* National Geographic, viewed 30 January 2020, <https://www.nationalgeographic.com/news/2018/02/neanderthals-cave-art-humans-evolution-science/>

Dias, S. F., and Nichols, K. 2020, *El Greco: Greek-Spanish Painter, Sculptor, and Architect,* Art Story, viewed 31 January 2020, <https://www.theartstory.org/artist/el-greco/>

Wethey, H. 2020, *El Greco: Spanish Artists*, Encyclopedia Britannica, viewed 31 January 2020, <https://www.britannica.com/biography/El-Greco>

Editors of the Encyclopedia Britannica 2019, *Francisco de Zurbaran,* Encyclopedia Britannica, viewed 31 January 2020, <https://www.britannica.com/biography/Francisco-de-Zurbaran>

Biography.com Editors 2019, *Diego Velázquez Biography,* A&E Television Networks, viewed 31 January 2020, <https://www.biography.com/artist/diego-Velázquez>

Adelson, B. M. 2005, *The Lives of Dwarfs: Their Journey from Public Curiosity Toward Social Liberation,* excerpted at POV.org,

viewed 31 January 2020,
<http://archive.pov.org/nobiggerthanaminute/diego-Velázquez/>

The Art Story Contributors 2020, *Bartolome Esteban Murillo,* The Art Story, viewed 31 January 2020,
<https://www.theartstory.org/artist/murillo-bartolome-esteban/life-and-legacy/>

Biography.com Editors 2019, *Francisco Goya Biography*, A&E Television Networks, viewed 31 January 2020,
<https://www.biography.com/artist/francisco-de-goya>

Stewart, J. 2019, *10 Surprising Facts about Pablo Picasso*, My Modern Met, viewed 3 February 2020,
<https://mymodernmet.com/surprising-pablo-picasso-facts/>

McCully, M. 2020, *Pablo Picasso: Spanish Artist*, Encyclopedia Britannica, viewed 3 February 2020,
<https://www.britannica.com/biography/Pablo-Picasso>

Artsy Editors, 2014, *Spanish Art History in a Nutshell*, Artsy, viewed 31 January 2020, <https://www.artsy.net/article/artsy-editorial-spanish-art-history-in-a-nutshell>

Gotthardt, A. 2017, *The Emotional Turmoil behind Picasso's Blue Period*, Artsy, viewed 3 February 2020,
<https://www.artsy.net/article/artsy-editorial-emotional-turmoil-picassos-blue-period>

Chernick, K. 2018, *The Ballets Russes Showcased Some of Picasso's and Matisse's Most Experimental Work*, Artsy, viewed 4 February 2020, <https://www.artsy.net/article/artsy-editorial-ballets-russes-showcased-picassos-matisses-experimental-work>

Polizzotti, M. 1995, *Revolution of the Mind: The Life of Andre Breton*, Washington Post, viewed 4 February 2020,
<https://www.washingtonpost.com/wp-srv/style/longterm/books/chap1/revoluti.htm>

History.com Editors 2018, *Surrealism History*, A&E Television Networks, viewed 3 February 2020,
<https://www.history.com/topics/art-history/surrealism-history>

Mann, J 2016, *How the Surrealist Movement Shaped the Course of Art History*, Artsy, viewed 3 February 2020, <https://www.artsy.net/article/artsy-editorial-what-is-surrealism>

Puchko, K. 2018, *15 Things You Didn't Know About the Persistence of Memory*, Mental Floss, viewed 5 February 2020, <https://www.mentalfloss.com/article/62725/15-things-you-didnt-know-about-persistence-memory>

Federal Bureau of Investigation, *Lindbergh Kidnapping*, FBI.gov, viewed 5 February 2020, <https://www.fbi.gov/history/famous-cases/lindbergh-kidnapping>

Jones, J. 2018, *When The Surrealists Expelled Salvador Dalí for "The Glorification of Hitlerian Fascism"*, Open Culture, viewed 5 February 2020, <http://www.openculture.com/2018/03/when-the-surrealists-expelled-salvador-Dalí-for-the-glorification-of-hitlerian-fascism-1934.html>

Valjak, D. 2017, *Salvador Dalí was expelled from the surrealist community for being fascinated with Hitler*, The Vintage News, viewed 5 February 2020, <https://www.thevintagenews.com/2017/01/04/salvador-Dalí-was-expelled-from-the-surrealist-community-for-being-fascinated-with-hitler/>

Blumberg, N. 2020, *Julien Levy: American Art Dealer*, Encyclopedia Britannica, viewed 5 February 2020, <https://www.britannica.com/biography/Julien-Levy>

Pollard, J. & Pollard, S. 2018, *The London International Surrealists Exhibition*, History Today, viewed 5 February 2020, <https://www.historytoday.com/archive/months-past/london-international-surrealists-exhibition>

Fitzgerald, M. 2014, *A Relationship Fraught and Fruitful*, The Wall Street Journal, viewed 3 February 2020, <https://www.wsj.com/articles/a-relationship-fraught-and-fruitful-on-picasso-Dalí-Dalí-picasso-at-the-Dalí-museum-1419982238>

Kassam, A. 2015, *Federico Garcia Lorca was killed on official orders, say 1960s police files*, The Guardian, viewed 6 February 2020,

<https://www.theguardian.com/culture/2015/apr/23/federico-garcia-lorca-spanish-poet-killed-orders-spanish-civil-war>

The Editors of the Encyclopedia Britannica 2016, *Blood Wedding: Play by Garcia Lorca*, Encyclopedia Britannica, viewed 6 February 2020, <https://www.britannica.com/topic/Blood-Wedding>

Santos Toroella, R. 2019, *When Dalí made up with his Father*, Mirador, viewed 6 February 2020, <https://www.miradorarts.com/when-Dalí-made-up-with-his-father/>

Rothman, L. and Ronk, L. 2016, *See 10 of the Most Surreal Portraits of Salvador Dalí*, Time Magazine, viewed 6 February 2020, <https://time.com/4318151/salvador-Dalí/>

Poetry Foundation, *Federico Garcia Lorca*, viewed 6 February 2020, <https://www.poetryfoundation.org/poets/federico-garcia-lorca>

Cartwright, M. 2017, *Narcissus*, Ancient History Encyclopedia, viewed 6 February 2020, <https://www.ancient.eu/Narcissus/>

Gallagher, P. 2020, *That Time Salvador Dalí Met Sigmund Freud*, Dangerous Minds, viewed 6 February 2020, <https://dangerousminds.net/comments/that_time_salvador_Dalí_met_sigmund_freud>

Cherry, K. 2020, *Sigmund Freud's Life and Contributions to Psychology*, Verywell Mind, viewed 6 February 2020, <https://www.verywellmind.com/sigmund-freud-biography-1856-1939-2795544>

Richman-Abdou, K. 2019, *Exploring Salvador Dalí's Strange and Surreal 'Persistence of Memory'*, My Modern Met, viewed 4 February 2020, <https://mymodernmet.com/the-persistence-of-memory-salvador-Dalí/2/>

Biography.com Editors 2019, *Coco Chanel Biography*, A&E Television Networks, viewed 6 February 2020, <https://www.biography.com/fashion-designer/coco-chanel>

Chimera, P. 1989, *A Broken Window 50 Years Ago Put Dalí on Main Street*, The Buffalo News, viewed 6 February 2020, <https://buffalonews.com/1989/05/04/a-broken-window-50-years-ago-put-Dalí-on-main-street/>

Aguer, M. 2019, *Creating a Surrealist Experiment: Dalí's 'Dream of Venus' at World Expo 1939 New York*, Bureau International des Expositions, viewed 6 February 2020, <https://www.bie-paris.org/site/en/blog/entry/creating-a-surrealist-experiment-salvador-Dalí-s-dream-of-venus-at-world-expo-1939-new-york>

History.com Editors 2019, *World War II*, A&E Television Networks, viewed 6 February 2020, <https://www.history.com/topics/world-war-ii/world-war-ii-history>

Anonymous 2016, *"When You've Got It, Flaunt It": Salvador Dalí's Success in Commercial America*, Explosion in a Shingle Factory, viewed 7 February 2020, <https://explosioninashinglefactory.wordpress.com/2016/08/02/when-youve-got-it-flaunt-it/>

Sorene, P. 2016, *When Salvador Dalí Made Alice Cooper's Brain From Ants and an Eclair (1973)*, Flashbak, viewed 7 February 2020, <https://flashbak.com/when-salvador-Dalí-made-alice-coopers-brain-from-ants-and-an-eclair-1973-361574/>

Lissack, S. 2014, *Dalí in Holographic Space*, Spie, viewed 7 February 2020, <https://spie.org/news/spie-professional-magazine-archive/2014-january/Dalí-in-holographic-space?SSO=1>

Ruiz, C. 2010, *Salvador Dalí and science, beyond mere curiosity*, Centre for Dalínian Studies, viewed 7 February 2020, <https://www.salvador-Dalí.org/media/upload/pdf/salvador-Dalí-and-science_1409303010.pdf>

History.com Editors 2019, *Spanish Civil War breaks out*, A&E Television Networks, viewed 5 February 2020, <https://www.history.com/this-day-in-history/spanish-civil-war-breaks-out>

Stanska, Z. 2017, *Dalí and Gala – The Love Story*, Daily Art Magazine, viewed January and February 2020, <https://www.dailyartmagazine.com/Dalí-gala-great-love-story/>

Minder, R. 2018, *Gala Dalí's Life Wasn't Quite Surreal, but It Was Pretty Strange*, The New York Times, viewed January and February 2020,

<https://www.nytimes.com/2018/07/25/arts/design/gala-salvador-Dalí-exhibition.html>

Dalí Universe Team 2017, *Dalí in New York*, Dalí Universe, viewed January and February 2020, <https://www.theDalíuniverse.com/en/news-Dalí-new-york>

Milliman, H. 2019, *Gala Dalí: Salvador Dalí's Demon Bride*, Museum Hack, viewed 7 February 2020, <https://museumhack.com/gala-Dalí/>

The Editors of the Encyclopedia Britannica 2020, *Juan Carlos: King of Spain*, Encyclopedia Britannica, viewed 7 February 2020, <https://www.britannica.com/biography/Juan-Carlos>

Burns, T. 1984, *The Dalí Drama*, The Washington Post, viewed 7 February 2020, <https://www.washingtonpost.com/archive/lifestyle/1984/09/11/the-Dalí-drama/eb173081-3dad-46a4-a719-87577deee4d2/>

Sinclair, K. 2017, *How did Salvador Dalí's mustache survive his death?*, Science Magazine, viewed 7 February 2020, <https://www.sciencemag.org/news/2017/07/how-did-salvador-dal-s-mustache-survive-his-death>

Rodríguez, M. 2017, *Judge dismissed Dalí paternity suit, orders plaintiff to pay costs*, El Pais, viewed 7 February 2020, <https://english.elpais.com/elpais/2017/10/16/inenglish/1508162182_382972.html>

Held, A. 2017, *Exhumation Show Spanish Woman Not Salvador Dalí's Daughter, Foundation Says*, NPR, viewed 7 February 2020, <https://www.npr.org/sections/thetwo-way/2017/09/06/548934012/exhumation-shows-spanish-woman-not-salvador-dal-s-daughter-says-foundation>

Kennedy, M. and Jones, S. 2017, *Court orders Salvador Dalí's body be exhumed for paternity test*, The Guardian, viewed 7 February 2020, <https://www.theguardian.com/world/2017/jun/26/court-orders-salvador-Dalí-body-be-exhumed-for-paternity-test-dna-claim-woman-surrealist-artist-spain>

Jones, S. 2017, *Salvador Dalí reburied after exhumation for paternity tests*, The Guardian, viewed 7 February 2020, <https://www.theguardian.com/artanddesign/2018/mar/16/salvador-Dalí-reburied-after-exhumation-for-paternity-tests>

Hedgecoe, G. 2017, *Digging up Dalí: Why experts question artist paternity claim*, BBC News, viewed 7 February 2020, <https://www.bbc.com/news/world-europe-40653883>

Epstein, R. 2016, *Jeff Koons*, The Art Story, viewed 7 February 2020, <https://www.theartstory.org/artist/koons-jeff/>

Anonymous 2018, *Salvador Dalí*, History-Biography.com, viewed January and February 2020, <https://history-biography.com/salvador-Dalí/>

Anonymous 2009, *Artist of the Day - Salvador Dalí*, A Different Kind of Blog, viewed January and February 2020, <https://tothewire.wordpress.com/2009/07/29/artist-of-the-day-salvador-Dalí/>

The Art Story Contributors 2011, *Salvador Dalí - Biography and Legacy*, The Art Story, viewed January and February 2020, <https://www.theartstory.org/artist/Dalí-salvador/life-and-legacy/>

Stewart, J. 2019, *18 Surreal Facts About Salvador Dalí*, My Modern Met, viewed January and February 2020, <https://mymodernmet.com/salvador-Dalí-facts/2/>

Biography.com Editors 2020, *Salvador Dalí Biography*, A&E Television Networks, viewed January and February 2020, <https://www.biography.com/artist/salvador-Dalí>

The Editors of the Encyclopedia Britannica 2020, *Salvador Dalí: Spanish Artist*, Encyclopedia Britannica, viewed January and February 2020, <https://www.britannica.com/biography/Salvador-Dalí>

Illustration I: By Carl Van Vechten - Library of CongressCatalog: http://lccn.loc.gov/2004662765Image download: http://cdn.loc.gov/service/pnp/van/5a51000/5a51800/5a51874r.jpgOriginal url: https://www.loc.gov/pictures/item/2004662765/, Public Domain, https://commons.wikimedia.org/w/index.php?curid=66144375

Illustration II: By Диана Бобрович - Own work, CC BY-SA 4.0, https://commons.wikimedia.org/w/index.php?curid=85917277

Illustration III: https://commons.wikimedia.org/wiki/File:Salvador-Dalí-salvador-Dalí-siurrealizm-kartina-metamorfoza.jpg

Illustration IV: https://upload.wikimedia.org/wikipedia/commons/2/27/Salvador_Dalí_NYWTS.jpg

Illustration V: https://commons.wikimedia.org/wiki/File:Teater_Museu_Gala_Salvador_Dalí_building_from_outside.jpg

www.ingramcontent.com/pod-product-compliance
Lightning Source LLC
LaVergne TN
LVHW041645060526
838200LV00040B/1720